Raspberry Pi Command Line: The Raspberry Pi terminal guide

First Edition
Sarful Hassan

Preface

The Raspberry Pi has revolutionized computing, offering a powerful, low-cost platform that anyone can use to learn programming, hardware integration, and Linux command-line operations. This book, *Raspberry Pi Command Line: The Raspberry Pi Terminal Guide*, is designed for both beginners and intermediate users who want to fully unlock the potential of the Raspberry Pi by mastering its command line interface. Through comprehensive and practical instructions, this guide provides everything needed to explore the terminal and get hands-on with your device.

Who This Book Is For

This book is intended for Raspberry Pi enthusiasts of all skill levels who are interested in mastering command-line operations on their devices. It is especially beneficial for those who wish to gain a deeper understanding of Linux systems, perform automation, and harness the power of the Raspberry Pi for projects involving programming, networking, and hardware control. If you're a student, hobbyist, or professional looking to expand your Raspberry Pi skills, this guide is for you.

How This Book Is Organized

This book is divided into chapters, each focusing on specific areas of command-line operations for the Raspberry Pi:

1. Introduction to essential concepts of the command line.
2. Navigation, file management, and basic networking.
3. Advanced topics like security, permissions, system monitoring, and more.

Each chapter includes practical examples and tips to deepen your understanding.

What Was Left Out

While we aim to cover all major command-line tools and functions available on the Raspberry Pi, some advanced programming and development topics have been left out to keep the book accessible for beginners. Topics such as advanced scripting and in-depth hardware programming are beyond the scope but are worth exploring as a next step.

Code Style (About the Code)

Code examples in this book follow a simple and consistent style, ensuring they are easy to read and understand. Commands and code snippets are presented in a monospaced font, and each example includes comments where necessary to explain its purpose and usage. Always type the code exactly as shown to avoid errors, and remember that Linux commands are case-sensitive.

Release Notes

This edition has been thoroughly revised to incorporate the latest features of the Raspberry Pi OS and includes updates on command-line tools. We've refined each chapter to include up-to-date examples and address user feedback from the previous edition.

Notes on the First Edition

The first edition of this book was a successful introduction to the world of Raspberry Pi command-line operations. This new edition expands on the fundamentals with additional topics, improved explanations, and a user-friendly approach based on feedback from readers.

MechatronicsLAB Online Learning

MechatronicsLAB is committed to providing high-quality resources for learning about Raspberry Pi, embedded systems, and mechatronics. For additional resources, tutorials, and courses, please visit our website or contact us directly.

How to Contact Us

- Email: mechatronicslab@gmail.com
- Website: mechatronicslab.net

Acknowledgments for the First Edition
We would like to thank our readers and contributors for their invaluable feedback, which helped shape this book. Special thanks to the Raspberry Pi community for their dedication to open-source knowledge and support.

Copyright

Disclaimer
The information provided in this book is for educational purposes only. While we have made every effort to ensure the accuracy of information, MechatronicsLAB does not assume any liability for errors or omissions. Readers are encouraged to consult official Raspberry Pi documentation for the latest updates and practices.

Table of Contents

Chapter- 1 Introduction to Raspberry Pi Command Line

Chapter Overview

The command line is a powerful tool that lets you interact with your Raspberry Pi by typing in commands. While the Raspberry Pi has a regular desktop interface, using the command line can make some tasks faster and more flexible. In this chapter, we'll explain what the command line is, why it's useful, basic rules for using it effectively, how to use shortcuts, and how to set up access either directly on the Raspberry Pi or from another computer.

Chapter Goal

- Understand what the Raspberry Pi command line is and why it's useful.
- Learn the primary rules and shortcuts for using the command line.
- Set up access to the command line on the Raspberry Pi, either directly or remotely.

What is the Raspberry Pi Command Line?

The **command line** (also known as the **terminal** or **shell**) is a way to control your Raspberry Pi by typing in instructions rather than clicking on icons or menus. You type in text commands to get the computer to do something, like listing files or installing software.

The Raspberry Pi command line uses a program called **Bash** (which stands for Bourne Again SHell). When you open the terminal, you'll see a prompt (often ending in $) where you can start typing commands.

Basic Terms

- **Command**: An instruction you give the computer. For example, typing `ls` and pressing Enter will show you a list of files.
- **Shell**: The program that reads and runs your commands. On Raspberry Pi, this is usually Bash.
- **Terminal**: The window where you type your commands. This is often referred to as the "command line."

Simple Commands to Get Started

Here are a few basic commands you can try:

- `ls` – Lists files and folders.
- `cd foldername` – Changes the current directory to a different folder.
- `mkdir foldername` – Creates a new folder.
- `rm filename` – Deletes a file.

1.2 Why Use the Command Line?

The command line may seem intimidating at first, but it's actually very useful. Here are some reasons why the command line can be helpful:

1.2.1 Faster for Many Tasks

Some tasks are faster to do with the command line than with a mouse. For example, if you want to install a new program, you can type a single command instead of clicking through several menus.

1.2.2 Automate Tasks

You can use the command line to create **scripts**, which are files that contain multiple commands. Scripts are great for automating tasks that you do repeatedly, like making backups or running tests.

1.2.3 Access to Advanced Tools

Some tools and settings on the Raspberry Pi are only available in the command line. This includes things like checking your network status, updating the system, or setting up hardware.

1.2.4 Use Fewer Resources

The command line uses less memory and processing power than a graphical interface, so your Raspberry Pi can run more efficiently, especially for tasks that don't need a screen or mouse.

1.2.5 Remote Access

The command line allows you to control your Raspberry Pi from another computer using **SSH** (Secure Shell). This means you don't need to connect a screen, keyboard, or mouse directly to the Pi; you can use your laptop to connect over a network instead.

1.3 Rules for Using the Command Line

To use the command line effectively, here are some basic rules to follow. These rules help you use the command line safely and prevent mistakes.

1.3.1 Think Before You Type

Commands run instantly, so always double-check before pressing Enter. Some commands can delete or modify files, so be sure you understand what a command does.

1.3.2 Use Sudo Only When Necessary

`sudo` is a command that gives you administrative (root) access, allowing you to make significant changes to your Raspberry Pi. Use it carefully; avoid using `sudo` unless you're certain you need it.

1.3.3 Be Careful with File Deletion

Deleting files from the command line with `rm` or `rmdir` is permanent. These commands don't send files to the trash; once deleted, they can't be recovered. Always check the file name and path before deleting.

1.3.4 Use Help and Man Pages

If you're not sure what a command does, you can use `man` (short for "manual") to learn more. Type `man command_name` (e.g., `man ls`) to see the command's manual. You can also use `command --help` to see quick options for a command.

1.3.5 Stay in Your Home Directory

The **home directory** is where your personal files are stored. It's safer to stay here (in `/home/pi` or ~) when you're new to the command line. Moving out of this directory without knowing where you are can lead to accidentally changing or deleting important system files.

1.3.6 Keep Commands Simple at First

When you're just starting out, keep your commands simple. Try basic commands like `ls`, `cd`, and `mkdir` before moving to more complex ones. This will help you get comfortable with the command line.

1.3.7 Save Scripts Before Running

If you're using a script to run multiple commands, save your work often and review the script before running it. Scripts can execute several commands in a row, so it's essential to make sure everything is correct.

1.4 Using Shortcuts in the Command Line

Learning a few command line shortcuts can make working with the terminal much faster and easier. Here are some common shortcuts to help you work more efficiently:

1.4.1 Tab Completion

- **Tab**: When typing a file or folder name, press **Tab** to automatically complete it.
    - Example: Typing `cd Doc` and pressing **Tab** will complete the name to `cd Documents` if there's a folder called "Documents."

1.4.2 Navigating Command History

- **Up Arrow**: Press the **Up Arrow** to scroll through previous commands you've used. This is useful if you need to repeat or edit a command.
- **Down Arrow**: Press the **Down Arrow** to scroll forward through your command history.

1.4.3 Clearing the Screen

- **Ctrl + L**: Pressing **Ctrl + L** clears the terminal screen, giving you a clean slate without deleting the previous output.

1.4.4 Canceling Commands

- **Ctrl + C**: If you start a command by mistake or it's taking too long to run, press **Ctrl + C** to cancel it. This can stop a running command or script.

1.4.5 Jumping to the Start or End of a Line

- **Ctrl + A**: Move the cursor to the beginning of the current line.
- **Ctrl + E**: Move the cursor to the end of the current line.

1.4.6 Deleting Entire Lines or Words

- **Ctrl + U**: Delete everything from the cursor's current position back to the beginning of the line.
- **Ctrl + K**: Delete everything from the cursor's position to the end of the line.
- **Ctrl + W**: Delete the word before the cursor. This can be helpful for quickly fixing typos.

1.4.7 Repeating Previous Commands

- **!!**: Repeats the last command.
  - Example: Typing `!!` and pressing Enter will rerun the last command.
- **!command**: Repeat the most recent command that starts with a specific word.
  - Example: `!ls` will rerun the last `ls` command.

Using these shortcuts can help you navigate and manage the command line more efficiently, allowing you to focus more on your work and less on typing.

1.5 Setting Up Access: Keyboard and Monitor or SSH

There are two main ways to access the command line on the Raspberry Pi:

1. By connecting a keyboard, mouse, and monitor directly to the Raspberry Pi.
2. By connecting to the Raspberry Pi from another computer using **SSH** (Secure Shell), which lets you control the Pi remotely.

1.5.1 Accessing the Command Line with Keyboard and Monitor

To access the command line directly on the Raspberry Pi:

1. **Connect your hardware**:
   - o Plug in a USB keyboard and mouse.
   - o Connect a monitor using an HDMI cable.
2. **Power up the Raspberry Pi**:
   - o Insert the microSD card (with Raspberry Pi OS installed) into the Pi.
   - o Plug in the power supply to turn on the Pi.
3. **Open the Terminal**:
   - o When the desktop loads, find the Terminal icon (it looks like a black square or may say "Terminal").
   - o Click on it to open a terminal window, where you can start typing commands.

You should see a prompt that looks like this:

```
pi@raspberrypi:~ $
```

Now you can start typing commands to interact with the Raspberry Pi.

1.5.2 Accessing the Command Line via SSH (Secure Shell)

SSH is a way to access the command line from another computer on the same network, which is helpful if you don't have a monitor or keyboard connected directly to the Raspberry Pi.

Step 1: Enable SSH on the Raspberry Pi

You can enable SSH from the Raspberry Pi desktop or command line.

From the Desktop:
1. Open the **Start Menu** by clicking the Raspberry Pi logo.
2. Go to **Preferences > Raspberry Pi Configuration**.
3. In the **Interfaces** tab, find **SSH** and set it to **Enabled**.
4. Click **OK** to save.

From the Command Line:
1. Open the terminal.
2. Type the following command and press Enter:

```
sudo raspi-config
```

3. Go to **Interfacing Options**, select **SSH**, and choose **Yes**.

Step 2: Find the Raspberry Pi's IP Address
To connect via SSH, you need the Raspberry Pi's IP address:

1. In the terminal, type:

```
hostname -I
```

2. This command will display your Pi's IP address, which looks like a series of numbers (e.g., `192.168.1.100`).

Step 3: Connect to the Raspberry Pi from Another Computer

Now, you can use an SSH client to connect. The steps differ slightly based on your computer:

On Linux/macOS:
1. Open the terminal.
2. Type the following, replacing `<IP_ADDRESS>` with your Pi's IP address:

```
ssh pi@<IP_ADDRESS>
```

3. Enter the Raspberry Pi password when prompted (the default is `raspberry`).

On Windows:
1. Download and open an SSH client like **PuTTY**.
2. Enter the Raspberry Pi's IP address in the **Host Name** field and select **Open**.
3. When prompted, enter the Raspberry Pi's password.

After logging in, you'll have access to the Raspberry Pi's command line from your computer.

Summary

In this chapter, we introduced the Raspberry Pi command line, explaining what it is and why it's useful. We covered some common ways to use the command line, basic rules and shortcuts for using it safely, and went over two methods for accessing the command line: directly with a keyboard and monitor or remotely using SSH. With command line access set up and some key rules and shortcuts in mind, you're ready to start exploring the Raspberry Pi through commands, making it easier to manage, automate, and control.

Chapter- 2 Basic Navigation and System Information

Chapter Overview

This chapter introduces essential commands for navigating the Raspberry Pi file system and accessing basic system information. These commands are fundamental tools for any Raspberry Pi user, helping you move between folders, view file locations, and check important details about your system's status, including disk space, memory, and uptime. Mastering these commands will provide a solid foundation for using the Raspberry Pi's command line.

Chapter Purpose

- **Learn foundational commands** to navigate the Raspberry Pi's file system.
- **View essential system information** such as disk space, memory, uptime, and the active user.
- **Understand system and user information** to manage resources efficiently.
- **Build confidence with the command line** for easier control over the Raspberry Pi.

Syntax Table

Topics	Syntax	Simple Example
Listing Files	`ls`	`ls`
Changing Directory	`cd <directory>`	`cd Documents`
Print Current Directory	`pwd`	`pwd`
System Information	`uname -a`	`uname -a`
Hostname	`hostname`	`hostname`
Disk Space	`df -h`	`df -h`
Memory Usage	`free -h`	`free -h`
System Uptime	`uptime`	`uptime`
Current User	`whoami`	`whoami`

Command Details

Listing Files

What is It?
The `ls` command lists all files and directories in your current location. It's similar to opening a folder on a graphical interface to see what's inside.

Use

- List files in the current directory.
- Display hidden files.
- Show additional file details, such as size and modification date.

Syntax

```
ls [options]
```

Syntax Explanation

- `ls`: The basic command for listing files and folders.
- **Options**:
    - `-l`: Displays detailed information about each file (e.g., permissions, owner, size, and last modified date).
    - `-a`: Shows hidden files (files beginning with a dot, such as `.config`).

Example

```
ls -l
```

Example Explanation

The `ls -l` command lists all files in the current directory, displaying additional information about each file. For example, you'll see file permissions (`drwxr-xr-x`), the owner, file size, and last modified date. This command helps you understand each file's properties and access permissions.

Changing Directory

What is It?

The `cd` command allows you to navigate between directories (folders), similar to double-clicking a folder to open it on a computer.

Use

- Enter a specific folder to access its contents.
- Move back to the previous directory.
- Access your home directory directly.

Syntax

```
cd <directory>
```

Syntax Explanation

- cd: Stands for "change directory."
- <directory>: Replace with the folder name you want to enter.
  - Use cd .. to move up one level in the directory structure.
  - Use cd ~ to go directly to your home directory.

Example

```
cd Documents
```

Example Explanation

This command moves you into the **Documents** folder. You can verify your location by typing pwd to see the current directory path.

Print Current Directory

What is It?

The pwd command shows the full path of your current directory, helping you know exactly where you are in the file system.

Use

- Confirm your current location within the directory structure.
- View the full path from the root directory to your current directory.

Syntax

```
pwd
```

Syntax Explanation

- pwd: Stands for "print working directory." This command shows the exact path from the root directory to your current location.

Example

```
pwd
```

Example Explanation

Typing pwd outputs the complete directory path, such as /home/pi/Documents, which shows your current location. This is particularly useful if you're working in deep directories and want to confirm your location.

System Information

What is It?

The uname -a command provides details about your Raspberry Pi's operating system and hardware, including the OS version, kernel version, and device architecture.

Use

- Check the operating system and kernel version.
- Identify the architecture (important for compatibility with software).
- Obtain detailed system information for troubleshooting.

Syntax

```
uname -a
```

Syntax Explanation

- uname: Command for basic system information.
- -a: Displays all available system details, including OS type, kernel version, and architecture.

Example

```
uname -a
```

Example Explanation

This command outputs details about the Raspberry Pi's OS, such as the kernel version (5.10.17-v7+), system architecture (armv7l), and other system information. This information can be helpful when installing software that requires specific system compatibility.

Hostname
What is It?

The hostname command displays the name of your Raspberry Pi on the network. This is useful if you have multiple devices connected to the same network.

Use

- Check your Raspberry Pi's network name.
- Set a new hostname for easy identification on the network.

Syntax

```
hostname [newhostname]
```

Syntax Explanation

- hostname: Shows or sets the device's name on the network.
- [newhostname]: (Optional) Enter a new name to change the hostname (requires sudo permission).

Example

```
hostname
```

Example Explanation

Typing hostname displays your device's current network name, making it easier to identify on a network with multiple devices. For example, if your device's hostname is raspberrypi, this command will display raspberrypi in the output.

Disk Space

What is It?

The df -h command displays the amount of disk space used and available on your system. It helps you monitor storage usage across your drives.

Use

- Check how much storage space is available.
- Monitor disk usage to prevent running out of space.
- View disk space on all mounted drives.

Syntax

```
df -h
```

Syntax Explanation

- df: Stands for "disk free," showing space usage.
- -h: Formats the output to be human-readable, with sizes in GB, MB, etc.

Example

```
df -h
```

Example Explanation
The df -h command displays disk space usage in a human-readable format. For each drive, you'll see the total, used, and available space, as well as the percentage used. This information is useful for managing storage, especially if you're working with limited disk space.

Memory Usage

What is It?
The free -h command shows the amount of memory (RAM) used and available, helping you monitor your system's memory usage, especially if running multiple applications.

Use

- Monitor available and used memory.
- Track memory usage to ensure sufficient resources for tasks.
- Identify if memory is a bottleneck for system performance.

Syntax

```
free -h
```

Syntax Explanation

- free: Command to display memory usage.
- -h: Formats the output to be human-readable, with sizes in GB, MB, etc.

Example

```
free -h
```

Example Explanation
The free -h command shows total, used, and available memory. For example, you might see output like 926M used and 605M available, which indicates how much memory is free for other tasks. Monitoring memory can be useful if your Pi starts to slow down or experiences performance issues.

System Uptime

What is It?

The `uptime` command shows how long your Raspberry Pi has been running since the last reboot, as well as system load averages indicating overall activity.

Use

- Check the duration the system has been running.
- Monitor system load for performance insights.
- Identify if the system has been running for extended periods.

Syntax

```
uptime
```

Syntax Explanation

- `uptime`: Displays the system uptime, current time, load averages, and the number of users logged in.

Example

```
uptime
```

Example Explanation

The `uptime` command shows the time since the last reboot, such as `3 days, 2 hours`. It also provides load averages, which indicate system activity. If the load average is high, it means the system has been working hard, which might suggest performance issues.

Current User

What is It?

The whoami command displays the username of the current user. It's especially useful if you're switching between accounts and need to confirm the active user.

Use

- Verify the active user account.
- Confirm user identity when switching between accounts.
- Double-check permissions for accessing files or commands.

Syntax

```
whoami
```

Syntax Explanation

- whoami: Stands for "who am I?" and outputs the current user's name.

Example

```
whoami
```

Example Explanation

Typing whoami shows the username of the active account. For example, if you're logged in as pi, this command outputs pi, confirming the current user. This is helpful in ensuring correct permissions, especially if you're working with multiple users.

Chapter Conclusion

These basic navigation and system information commands are foundational for any Raspberry Pi user. By mastering these commands, you'll be able to navigate the file system confidently, monitor system resources, and confirm system details. Practicing these commands will build your command-line skills and prepare you for more advanced tasks as you continue exploring your Raspberry Pi.

Chapter- 3 File and Directory Management

Chapter Overview

This chapter introduces key commands for managing files and directories on your Raspberry Pi. These commands help you create, delete, move, and locate files and folders, making it easier to organize and control the Raspberry Pi's file system. By mastering these commands, you'll be able to work with files efficiently on the command line.

Chapter Purpose

- **Learn to create and remove directories** for better file organization.
- **Understand how to copy, move, and rename files** within your Raspberry Pi.
- **Practice viewing and editing file content** with beginner-friendly commands.
- **Develop skills to locate files** quickly within your system.

Syntax Table

Topics	Syntax	Simple Example
Creating Directory	`mkdir <directory>`	`mkdir myfolder`
Removing Directory	`rmdir <directory>`	`rmdir myfolder`
Deleting File	`rm <file>`	`rm myfile.txt`
Copying Files	`cp <source> <destination>`	`cp file1.txt file2.txt`
Moving/Renaming Files	`mv <source> <destination>`	`mv oldname.txt newname.txt`
Displaying Content	`cat <filename>`	`cat myfile.txt`
Editing Files	`nano <filename>`	`nano myfile.txt`
Creating Empty File	`touch <filename>`	`touch newfile.txt`
Finding Files by Name	`find / -name <filename>`	`find / -name myfile.txt`
Quickly Locating Files	`locate <filename>`	`locate myfile.txt`

Command Details

Creating a Directory

What is It?

The `mkdir` command allows you to create a new directory (folder) in a specified location, which helps with organizing files by projects, types, or categories.

Use

- Create folders to organize files.
- Make multiple folders at once by specifying multiple names.
- Use in projects to keep related files together.

Syntax

```
mkdir <directory>
```

Syntax Explanation

- `mkdir`: Stands for "make directory."
- `<directory>`: Replace with the name of the folder you want to create.

Example

```
mkdir myfolder
```

Example Explanation

This command creates a folder named `myfolder` in your current directory. Use `ls` to confirm the new folder's creation.

Removing a Directory

What is It?
The `rmdir` command removes an empty directory. The directory must be empty before it can be deleted with this command.

Use

- Delete unused or empty directories.
- Organize the file system by removing unnecessary folders.
- Clean up temporary folders created for testing or organization.

Syntax

```
rmdir <directory>
```

Syntax Explanation

- `rmdir`: Stands for "remove directory."
- `<directory>`: Replace with the name of the folder you want to delete.

Example

```
rmdir myfolder
```

Example Explanation
This command deletes the folder named `myfolder`. If `myfolder` contains files, it will show an error, as the directory must be empty.

Deleting a File

What is It?
The `rm` command deletes a specified file. Use this command carefully, as it permanently removes files from the system.

Use

- Clear up space by removing unnecessary files.
- Delete outdated or incorrect files.
- Manage files by removing items you no longer need.

Syntax

```
rm <file>
```

Syntax Explanation

- rm: Stands for "remove."
- <file>: Replace with the name of the file you want to delete.

Example

```
rm myfile.txt
```

Example Explanation

This command deletes myfile.txt from the current directory. After running the command, type ls to verify the file has been deleted.

Copying Files

What is It?

The cp command copies a file from one location to another, creating an exact duplicate.

Use

- Create backup copies of important files.
- Duplicate files for editing without affecting the original.
- Copy files to another directory for better organization.

Syntax

```
cp <source> <destination>
```

Syntax Explanation

- cp: Stands for "copy."
- <source>: The file you want to copy.
- <destination>: The location where the copied file should go.

Example

```
cp file1.txt file2.txt
```

Example Explanation

This command copies file1.txt and names the duplicate file2.txt in the current directory. Use ls to confirm that file2.txt now exists.

Moving or Renaming Files

What is It?

The mv command moves a file to a different location or renames it. Moving is like cutting and pasting a file, while renaming changes the file's name within the same location.

Use

- Organize files by moving them to different folders.
- Rename files to maintain consistent naming conventions.
- Rearrange files into new directories.

Syntax

```
mv <source> <destination>
```

Syntax Explanation

- mv: Stands for "move."
- <source>: The file you want to move or rename.
- <destination>: The new location or name for the file.

Example

```
mv oldname.txt newname.txt
```

Example Explanation

This command renames oldname.txt to newname.txt. Type ls to confirm that the file's name has changed.

Displaying File Content

What is It?

The cat command displays the contents of a file directly in the terminal, making it ideal for quickly viewing small files.

Use

- Quickly view the content of text files.
- Check file content without editing.
- Display multiple files by listing them in sequence.

Syntax

```
cat <filename>
```

Syntax Explanation

- cat: Stands for "concatenate," commonly used to display file content.
- <filename>: The file you want to view.

Example

```
cat myfile.txt
```

Example Explanation

This command displays the entire content of myfile.txt in the terminal. It's useful for checking a file's contents without opening an editor.

Editing Files

What is It?

The nano command opens a file in the Nano text editor, a beginner-friendly and simple editor directly within the terminal.

Use

- Edit file content directly from the command line.
- Create and save changes to text files.
- Modify configuration files on your Raspberry Pi.

Syntax

```
nano <filename>
```

Syntax Explanation

- nano: Opens the Nano text editor.
- <filename>: The file you want to edit.

Example

```
nano myfile.txt
```

Example Explanation

This command opens myfile.txt in the Nano editor. After making changes, press Ctrl + X to exit, then Y to save your edits.

Creating an Empty File

What is It?

The `touch` command creates an empty file with the specified name. It's helpful for setting up new files or placeholders for future content.

Use

- Create new text files for future editing.
- Set up placeholder files for organizing projects.
- Update the modification time of an existing file.

Syntax

```
touch <filename>
```

Syntax Explanation

- `touch`: Creates a new, empty file.
- `<filename>`: The name of the file you want to create.

Example

```
touch newfile.txt
```

Example Explanation

This command creates an empty file named `newfile.txt`. Use `ls` to confirm the new file's presence in the directory.

Finding Files by Name

What is It?

The `find` command searches for files based on specific criteria, such as name or location. It's particularly useful for locating files in large directories or across the entire system.

Use

- Locate files anywhere in the file system.
- Search for files by name across the system.
- Narrow search results with additional options.

Syntax

```
find / -name <filename>
```

Syntax Explanation

- `find`: Command to search for files.
- `/`: Starting directory for the search (use / to search the entire system).
- `-name <filename>`: Replace <filename> with the name of the file you're looking for.

Example

```
find / -name myfile.txt
```

Example Explanation

This command searches the entire system for `myfile.txt`. The output shows the full path of any files matching the name, making it easier to locate files even in deep directories.

Quickly Locating File Paths

What is It?

The `locate` command quickly finds the paths of files using an index. This command is faster than `find` but may need to be installed on your Raspberry Pi.

Use

- Quickly locate files using a pre-built index.
- Avoid searching through the entire file system.
- Speed up file search with database-based indexing.

Syntax

```
locate <filename>
```

Syntax Explanation

- `locate`: Finds file paths using an index.
- `<filename>`: The name of the file you want to locate.

Example

```
locate myfile.txt
```

Example Explanation

This command finds and lists all paths for files named `myfile.txt`. It's a faster alternative to `find`, as it relies on an indexed database rather than searching each directory.

Tip: Run `sudo updatedb` to update the `locate` database if you recently added new files that need to be found.

Chapter Conclusion

These file and directory management commands provide essential tools for organizing and working with files on your Raspberry Pi. By learning to create, delete, move, and search for files, you gain greater control over your system's file structure. Practicing these commands regularly will help you become comfortable managing files and directories from the command line, building a solid foundation for more advanced file operations in future projects.

Chapter- 4 System Status and Monitoring

Chapter Overview

In this chapter, we'll explore essential commands for monitoring your Raspberry Pi's system status. These commands help you view real-time processes, check system temperature, and understand connected devices, giving you greater insight into your Raspberry Pi's performance and hardware status.

Chapter Purpose

- **Learn to monitor active processes** to understand resource usage.
- **Check system temperature and hardware information** to ensure optimal performance.
- **Identify connected devices** to manage USB and disk connections effectively.
- **Develop skills to troubleshoot** using system messages and logs.

Syntax Table

Topics	Syntax	Simple Example
Real-Time Process Monitoring	`top`	`top`
Listing All Processes	`ps aux`	`ps aux`
Advanced Process Monitor	`htop`	`htop`
Checking Temperature	`vcgencmd measure_temp`	`vcgencmd measure_temp`
Viewing System Messages	`dmesg`	`dmesg`
Listing USB Devices	`lsusb`	`lsusb`
Displaying CPU Information	`lscpu`	`lscpu`
Listing Block Devices	`lsblk`	`lsblk`

Command Details

Real-Time Process Monitoring

What is It?
The `top` command provides a real-time view of running processes, including their resource usage, such as CPU and memory consumption.

Use

- Monitor CPU and memory usage in real-time.
- Identify processes consuming high system resources.
- Track the system's overall load and performance.

Syntax

```
top
```

Syntax Explanation

- top: Opens an interactive view of active processes, refreshing every few seconds to show real-time usage.

Example

```
top
```

Example Explanation

This command shows a list of running processes, including the CPU and memory each process uses. By pressing q, you can exit the top interface. Use this command when you want a quick overview of your system's activity.

Listing All Processes
What is It?

The ps aux command lists all running processes along with detailed information, such as user, process ID (PID), CPU usage, and memory usage.

Use

- View all active processes.
- Check for specific processes that may need to be monitored or terminated.
- Troubleshoot by viewing processes that consume excessive resources.

Syntax

```
ps aux
```

Syntax Explanation

- ps: Stands for "process status."
- aux: Flags that display all processes, including those from other users and background processes.

Example

```
ps aux
```

Example Explanation

This command outputs a list of all processes with detailed information, which is useful for understanding each process's resource usage and state. You can use grep with ps aux to filter specific processes, e.g., ps aux | grep ssh.

Advanced Process Monitor

What is It?

The htop command is an advanced, interactive process monitor with a user-friendly interface. It displays processes and resource usage in a graphical format (requires installation).

Use

- Monitor system resources with an easy-to-read interface.
- Sort and filter processes interactively.
- View detailed information about each process with better control options.

Syntax

```
htop
```

Syntax Explanation

- `htop`: Launches an enhanced process monitor with colored output and interactive controls for managing processes.

Example

```
htop
```

Example Explanation

After running `htop`, you can navigate the interface to view details about each process. Use arrow keys to scroll and F10 to exit. This command offers a more intuitive process view than `top`.

Tip: If `htop` is not installed, you can install it with `sudo apt install htop`.

Checking Temperature

What is It?

The `vcgencmd measure_temp` command checks the Raspberry Pi's CPU temperature. Monitoring temperature is essential, especially if the Pi is running intensive tasks or is in an enclosed space.

Use

- Check if the Raspberry Pi is overheating.
- Monitor temperature during CPU-intensive tasks.
- Ensure optimal system cooling for longer device life.

Syntax

```
vcgencmd measure_temp
```

Syntax Explanation

- vcgencmd: A command to access various system parameters.
- measure_temp: Checks the current CPU temperature.

Example

```
vcgencmd measure_temp
```

Example Explanation

This command outputs the current temperature, such as temp=48.5'C. Maintaining a temperature below 80°C is recommended for optimal performance.

Viewing System Messages

What is It?

The dmesg command displays system messages and kernel logs. It's especially useful for debugging and understanding hardware interactions.

Use

- View recent system events and messages.
- Identify hardware-related issues or errors.
- Debug startup issues and kernel-related events.

Syntax

```
dmesg
```

Syntax Explanation

- dmesg: Stands for "diagnostic message," displaying recent messages generated by the kernel.

Example

```
dmesg
```

Example Explanation

This command outputs recent system messages, showing information about hardware interactions and events. Use `dmesg | tail` to view the latest messages or `dmesg | grep usb` to filter USB-related logs.

Listing USB Devices

What is It?

The `lsusb` command lists all USB devices currently connected to the Raspberry Pi. It helps you confirm USB connections, such as keyboards, drives, and network adapters.

Use

- Confirm which USB devices are connected.
- Troubleshoot USB device recognition issues.
- Identify connected devices for configuration purposes.

Syntax

```
lsusb
```

Syntax Explanation

- `lsusb`: Lists all connected USB devices and displays each device's vendor and product ID.

Example

```
lsusb
```

Example Explanation

Running `lsusb` shows a list of USB devices with vendor IDs, making it easy to identify specific connected devices. For example, you may see entries for keyboards, USB drives, or Wi-Fi adapters.

Displaying CPU Information

What is It?

The lscpu command provides information about the CPU architecture, such as the number of cores, model name, and CPU frequency.

Use

- Check CPU specifications for compatibility.
- Identify the number of cores and threads.
- Confirm CPU frequency and model for troubleshooting.

Syntax

```
lscpu
```

Syntax Explanation

- lscpu: Displays detailed information about the CPU, including model, architecture, and available cores.

Example

```
lscpu
```

Example Explanation

This command outputs CPU details like Model name, CPU(s), and MHz. The information helps you understand the CPU capabilities and can be useful when configuring software that depends on CPU specifications.

Listing Block Devices
What is It?

The lsblk command lists all block devices, such as connected hard drives, SSDs, SD cards, and USB storage devices. It's useful for viewing the storage devices and their partitions.

Use

- View connected storage devices.
- Confirm device mount points and partition sizes.
- Identify available storage devices for troubleshooting.

Syntax

```
lsblk
```

Syntax Explanation

- lsblk: Lists block devices and shows device names, sizes, types, and mount points.

Example

```
lsblk
```

Example Explanation

The command outputs a table of connected storage devices, including their size and mount location. For example, sda1 might represent a USB drive partition. This information helps you understand storage layout and available space.

Chapter Conclusion

These system status and monitoring commands allow you to keep an eye on your Raspberry Pi's health and performance. By mastering these commands, you'll be able to monitor active processes, check CPU temperature, and view connected devices effectively. Practicing these commands will help you maintain optimal performance and troubleshoot issues, ensuring your Raspberry Pi runs smoothly.

Chapter- 5 Basic Networking

Chapter Overview

This chapter covers essential networking commands that allow you to manage, test, and troubleshoot network connections on your Raspberry Pi. These commands help you view network configurations, test connectivity, scan for Wi-Fi networks, and download data from the internet. Understanding and practicing these basic networking commands ensures reliable connectivity and helps troubleshoot network issues effectively.

Chapter Purpose

- **View and manage network settings** to configure and monitor network interfaces.
- **Test network connectivity** for troubleshooting connection issues.
- **Fetch and download data** from online resources.
- **Scan and connect to Wi-Fi networks** to maintain a stable connection.

Syntax Table

Topics	Syntax	Simple Example
Network Configuration	`ifconfig` or `ip a`	`ifconfig`
Testing Network Connection	`ping <hostname or IP>`	`ping google.com`

Fetching Data from URL	`curl <URL>`	`curl http://example.co m`
Downloading Files	`wget <URL>`	`wget http://example.co m/file`
Displaying IP Address	`hostname -I`	`hostname -I`
Scanning Wi-Fi Networks	`iwlist wlan0 scan`	`iwlist wlan0 scan`
Checking Internet Connection	`ping google.com`	`ping google.com`

Command Details

Network Configuration

What is It?

The `ifconfig` command displays network configuration settings for each network interface on your Raspberry Pi, such as IP addresses, MAC addresses, and network interface statuses. The `ip a` command is a more modern replacement and may be used on newer systems.

Use

- **View IP addresses** for Ethernet (`eth0`) and Wi-Fi (`wlan0`) interfaces.
- **Check MAC addresses** for network configuration.
- **Verify connection status** of network interfaces.

Syntax

```
ifconfig
```

or

```
ip a
```

Syntax Explanation

- `ifconfig`: Lists each network interface and its IP, MAC address, and other network parameters.
- `ip a`: An alternative to `ifconfig` on some systems, with similar output.

Example

```
ifconfig
```

Example Explanation

This command outputs information for each network interface, showing IP addresses under `inet`, the MAC address, and current connection status. Look under `wlan0` or `eth0` to view the IP address assigned to each interface. You can use `ifconfig wlan0 down` and `ifconfig wlan0 up` to disable and enable the Wi-Fi interface as needed.

Testing Network Connection

What is It?

The `ping` command checks network connectivity to a specified hostname or IP address by sending small packets and measuring the response time. This command is essential for diagnosing network problems, as it reveals connectivity status and latency.

Use

- **Test connectivity** to another device or website.
- **Diagnose network delays** by observing response times.
- **Check packet loss** to identify unstable connections.

Syntax

```
ping <hostname or IP>
```

Syntax Explanation

- `ping`: Sends packets to the specified hostname or IP address.
- `<hostname or IP>`: The destination to test connectivity (e.g., `google.com` or a local device IP like `192.168.1.1`).

Example

```
ping google.com
```

Example Explanation

This command sends packets to `google.com` and measures the response time for each packet. If the connection is successful, you'll see response times for each packet; if it fails, it indicates connectivity issues. Press `Ctrl + C` to stop the ping test.

Tip: A high response time or packet loss indicates a possible network issue. Use `ping` on local network devices (e.g., `ping 192.168.1.1`) to test your LAN connection separately.

Fetching Data from a URL

What is It?

The `curl` command retrieves data from a specified URL, commonly used to test network connectivity, fetch web content, or interact with web APIs.

Use

- **Test if a website or API** is accessible.
- **Retrieve data** from a URL without a browser.
- **Fetch API responses** for testing or development purposes.

Syntax

```
curl <URL>
```

Syntax Explanation

- `curl`: Command to retrieve data from a URL and display it in the terminal.
- `<URL>`: The web address to fetch data from.

Example

```
curl http://example.com
```

Example Explanation

This command fetches and displays the content from example.com. If successful, you'll see the HTML content of the site in the terminal, which confirms network connectivity. If the URL is unreachable, `curl` will output an error message.

Tip: Use `curl -I <URL>` to fetch only the HTTP headers, which gives a quick network response without loading full content.

Downloading Files from a URL

What is It?

The `wget` command downloads files from a specified URL, making it easy to retrieve software packages, documents, or other files directly to your Raspberry Pi.

Use

- **Download files** from the internet for local access.
- **Retrieve software packages** for installation.
- **Save documents or images** from web sources.

Syntax

```
wget <URL>
```

Syntax Explanation

- wget: Downloads the specified file and saves it to the current directory.
- <URL>: The web address of the file to download.

Example

```
wget http://example.com/file.txt
```

Example Explanation

This command downloads file.txt from example.com and saves it in your current directory. Use ls to confirm the file has been downloaded. If the download fails, it might indicate a network issue.

Tip: Use wget -O <filename> <URL> to specify a custom name for the downloaded file.

Displaying IP Address

What is It?

The hostname -I command displays the IP address of your Raspberry Pi. This command provides a quick way to check your local IP address without viewing full network details.

Use

- **See your Pi's IP address** on the local network.
- **Identify the IP address** for SSH access or network configuration.
- **Check connectivity status** by verifying the IP assignment.

Syntax

```
hostname -I
```

Syntax Explanation

- hostname: A command related to network and host configurations.
- -I: Displays only the IP address assigned to the device.

Example

```
hostname -I
```

Example Explanation

This command shows your Pi's IP address, such as 192.168.1.5, which is helpful for connecting to your Raspberry Pi via SSH or configuring network settings.

Tip: Use ip route for additional networking details, including default gateway information.

Scanning Wi-Fi Networks

What is It?

The iwlist wlan0 scan command scans for available Wi-Fi networks, displaying details like network names (SSIDs), security protocols, and signal strength. This is helpful for finding and choosing the best network to connect to.

Use

- **Identify nearby Wi-Fi networks** and their SSIDs.
- **Check network signal strength** to choose the best option.
- **View security settings** to ensure compatibility with your Pi.

Syntax

```
iwlist wlan0 scan
```

Syntax Explanation

- `iwlist`: A command used for scanning wireless networks.
- `wlan0`: Specifies the Wi-Fi interface to scan (usually `wlan0` on the Raspberry Pi).
- `scan`: Option to initiate a Wi-Fi scan.

Example

```
iwlist wlan0 scan
```

Example Explanation

This command lists all available Wi-Fi networks, showing details like SSID (network name), signal strength, and security settings (WPA/WPA2). This information helps you select a network based on signal quality and security compatibility.

Tip: If the `wlan0` interface is not available, check network interfaces using `ifconfig` or `ip a`.

Checking Internet Connection

What is It?

The `ping google.com` command tests if your Raspberry Pi can reach the internet by pinging Google's servers. This is a quick test to confirm that the Pi has a working internet connection.

Use

- **Verify active internet connection** by checking if the Pi can reach Google.
- **Identify network delays** by observing response times.
- **Troubleshoot internet issues** by testing an external connection.

Syntax

```
ping google.com
```

Syntax Explanation

- `ping`: Sends packets to the specified hostname and waits for a response.
- `google.com`: A commonly-used server for internet connectivity testing.

Example

```
ping google.com
```

Example Explanation

This command sends packets to Google's server. If the connection is successful, you'll see response times in milliseconds. This output confirms that the Raspberry Pi has internet access. If the connection fails, it may indicate network or internet issues.

Tip: Use `ping -c 4 google.com` to limit the ping test to 4 packets for a quick check.

Chapter Conclusion

These basic networking commands are essential for managing and troubleshooting network connections on your Raspberry Pi. By mastering these commands, you'll be able to view network configurations, test connectivity, download files, and scan for available Wi-Fi networks. Regular practice with these commands will enable you to maintain reliable network connections, diagnose network issues, and ensure your Raspberry Pi stays connected to the internet and your local network effectively.

Chapter- 6 Software Management

Chapter Overview

This chapter introduces essential software management commands
for your Raspberry Pi. These commands help you keep your
software up to date, install and remove packages, and search for
available software. Mastering these commands ensures that your
system stays updated and optimized.

Chapter Purpose

- **Learn to update and upgrade software packages** to keep
  the system secure and efficient.
- **Install specific packages** as needed for different projects.
- **Remove unwanted packages** to free up system resources.
- **Search for available packages** to explore new software
  options.

Syntax Table

Topics	Syntax	Simple Example
Updating Package List	`sudo apt update`	`sudo apt update`
Upgrading Installed Packages	`sudo apt upgrade`	`sudo apt upgrade`
Installing a Package	`sudo apt install <package-name>`	`sudo apt install htop`

Removing a Package	`sudo apt remove <package-name>`	`sudo apt remove htop`
Listing Installed Packages	`dpkg -l`	`dpkg -l`
Searching for a Package	`apt search <package>`	`apt search python3`

Command Details

Updating Package List

What is It?

The `sudo apt update` command updates the package list, allowing your Raspberry Pi to retrieve information about the latest versions of available software. This is essential to ensure that any software installed or updated is the most recent version.

Use

- **Check for the latest available packages** from your configured sources.
- **Synchronize the package list** to prepare for upgrades or new installations.
- **Refresh software sources** for accurate package availability.

Syntax

```
sudo apt update
```

Syntax Explanation

- `sudo`: Grants root privileges, required for managing system packages.
- `apt`: The package management tool used on Debian-based systems, including Raspberry Pi OS.
- `update`: Option to refresh the list of available packages and versions.

Example

```
sudo apt update
```

Example Explanation

Running sudo apt update updates the package list from the repositories configured on your Raspberry Pi. This command does not install or upgrade software but simply updates the list of available packages.

Tip: It's recommended to run sudo apt update before installing new software to ensure you're getting the latest version.

Upgrading Installed Packages

What is It?

The sudo apt upgrade command upgrades installed packages to their latest versions based on the current package list. This command installs security patches, performance improvements, and new features for your existing software.

Use

- **Apply updates** to improve software security and stability.
- **Get the latest features** of installed applications.
- **Keep the system up to date** with minimal effort.

Syntax

```
sudo apt upgrade
```

Syntax Explanation

- sudo: Executes the command with root privileges.
- apt: The package management tool for Debian-based systems.
- upgrade: Installs the newest versions of installed packages based on the package list.

Example

```
sudo apt upgrade
```

Example Explanation

This command updates all installed packages to their latest versions, based on the most recent package list. You'll often see a summary of packages that will be upgraded, allowing you to confirm before proceeding.

Tip: For a full system upgrade that includes new packages required by the updates, use `sudo apt full-upgrade`.

Installing a Package

What is It?

The `sudo apt install <package-name>` command installs a specific package. This command is essential for adding new software to your Raspberry Pi, whether it's for development, utilities, or other functions.

Use

- **Install new software** required for specific tasks or projects.
- **Add utilities** for system monitoring, file management, or networking.
- **Install dependencies** for software development.

Syntax

```
sudo apt install <package-name>
```

Syntax Explanation

- `sudo`: Runs the command with root privileges.
- `apt`: The package manager.
- `install`: The option to install new packages.
- `<package-name>`: The name of the package you want to install (replace `<package-name>` with the actual package name).

Example

```
sudo apt install htop
```

Example Explanation

This command installs the htop package, a system monitoring tool. During installation, the package manager may prompt you to confirm, and then it will download and install the package and its dependencies.

Tip: To install multiple packages at once, list them after the command (e.g., sudo apt install htop nano curl).

Removing a Package

What is It?

The sudo apt remove <package-name> command uninstalls a specified package from your Raspberry Pi. Removing unused software frees up space and reduces system overhead.

Use

- **Uninstall software** that is no longer needed.
- **Clear up system resources** by removing unnecessary packages.
- **Keep the system organized** by removing unused packages.

Syntax

```
sudo apt remove <package-name>
```

Syntax Explanation

- sudo: Executes the command with root privileges.
- apt: The package manager.
- remove: The option to uninstall a specified package.
- <package-name>: The name of the package to remove.

Example

```
sudo apt remove htop
```

Example Explanation

This command removes the htop package. After entering the command, you'll see a summary and may be asked to confirm the removal. apt remove only removes the software itself but leaves configuration files intact.

Tip: To remove both the package and its configuration files, use sudo apt purge <package-name>.

Listing Installed Packages

What is It?

The dpkg -l command lists all packages currently installed on your Raspberry Pi, including system packages and applications. This command helps you check what software is already installed.

Use

- **Check for installed packages** on your Raspberry Pi.
- **Verify if a specific package** is already installed.
- **List all software** installed on the system.

Syntax

```
dpkg -l
```

Syntax Explanation

- dpkg: The lower-level package manager.
- -l: Option to list all installed packages.

Example

```
dpkg -l
```

Example Explanation
This command shows a table of installed packages, displaying each package's name, version, and status. The output can be extensive, so you may want to use dpkg -l | grep <package-name> to filter results for a specific package.

Tip: Use dpkg -s <package-name> to get detailed information about a specific package.

Searching for a Package

What is It?
The apt search <package> command searches the package repositories for software packages matching a specific term. This command is useful for finding software options or discovering new tools.

Use

- **Find available software** that meets specific needs.
- **Explore package options** for new tools or utilities.
- **Check if a package** exists in the repositories.

Syntax

```
apt search <package>
```

Syntax Explanation

- apt: The package manager.
- search: Option to search for packages in the repositories.
- <package>: The search term to find matching packages (replace <package> with the package name or keyword).

Example

```
apt search python3
```

Example Explanation

This command searches for packages related to python3. The output lists matching packages along with brief descriptions, helping you identify relevant options.

Tip: For more detailed information on a package, use apt show <package-name> after finding it with apt search.

Chapter Conclusion

These software management commands are essential for keeping your Raspberry Pi up to date, installing new software, and managing installed packages. By regularly updating and upgrading your system, you ensure better performance, security, and compatibility with newer applications. Practice using these commands to install, remove, and search for packages, and you'll be able to efficiently manage your Raspberry Pi's software environment.

Chapter- 7 User and Permissions Management

Chapter Overview

This chapter introduces essential commands for managing users and permissions on your Raspberry Pi. These commands allow you to create and manage user accounts, set permissions, assign group memberships, and control file ownership. Understanding user and permission management is crucial for ensuring the security and organization of your Raspberry Pi.

Chapter Purpose

- **Learn to add and manage users** to organize user accounts on your system.
- **Set and change passwords** to maintain account security.
- **Assign group memberships** to manage user permissions.
- **Configure file permissions and ownership** to control access to files.
- **Manage sudo privileges** for secure administrative access.

Syntax Table

Topics	Syntax	Simple Example
Adding a New User	adduser <username>	adduser john
Changing User Password	sudo passwd <username>	sudo passwd john

Adding User to Group	`sudo usermod -aG <group> <username>`	`sudo usermod -aG sudo john`
Showing User Groups	`groups`	`groups`
Changing File Permissions	`chmod <permissions> <file>`	`chmod 755 myfile.txt`
Changing File Owner/Group	`chown <user>:<group> <file>`	`chown john:staff myfile.txt`
Configuring Privileges	`sudo visudo`	`sudo visudo`

Command Details

Adding a New User

What is It?

The `adduser` command creates a new user account on your Raspberry Pi, along with a home directory and default configurations for that user.

Use

- **Add new users** to separate individual accounts.
- **Assign default settings** and home directories to new users.
- **Create distinct user profiles** for different access levels or roles.

Syntax

```
adduser <username>
```

Syntax Explanation

- `adduser`: Creates a new user and sets up the user's home directory and initial configurations.

- `<username>`: Replace with the name of the user you want to create.

Example

```
adduser john
```

Example Explanation

This command creates a new user named john. It prompts you for a password, full name, and other optional information, and then sets up the user's home directory at /home/john.

Tip: The adduser command offers a more user-friendly process than useradd, which is also available but requires more manual setup.

Changing User Password

What is It?

The sudo passwd `<username>` command allows you to set or change the password for a specified user, ensuring that only authorized users can access their accounts.

Use

- **Set or update user passwords** to maintain account security.
- **Reset forgotten passwords** for other users.
- **Enforce password changes** for improved security.

Syntax

```
sudo passwd <username>
```

Syntax Explanation

- sudo: Runs the command with root privileges, required for modifying user accounts.
- passwd: Command to change the password for a user.

- `<username>`: Replace with the user's name whose password you want to change.

Example

```
sudo passwd john
```

Example Explanation

This command sets or updates the password for the user john. You'll be prompted to enter and confirm the new password. This command can be used for any user, as long as you have root privileges.

Tip: Use strong, unique passwords for each user to enhance security.

Adding User to a Group

What is It?

The sudo usermod -aG <group> <username> command adds a specified user to an existing group, which is useful for managing permissions and access rights.

Use

- **Grant access to additional resources** by adding users to specific groups.
- **Assign permissions** through group memberships (e.g., adding to sudo group for admin rights).
- **Control access to files and directories** with group-based permissions.

Syntax

```
sudo usermod -aG <group> <username>
```

Syntax Explanation

- sudo: Grants root privileges to modify user settings.
- usermod: Command to modify a user's settings.
- -aG: Adds the user to a group without removing them from other groups.

- `<group>`: The name of the group to add the user to.
- `<username>`: The name of the user being added to the group.

Example

```
sudo usermod -aG sudo john
```

Example Explanation

This command adds the user john to the sudo group, allowing john to execute commands with root privileges. Adding a user to the sudo group is a common way to give them administrative rights.

Tip: Use groups `<username>` to check a user's current group memberships.

Showing User Groups

What is It?

The groups command displays the groups that the current user belongs to, which is helpful for verifying group memberships and permissions.

Use

- **View current user's group memberships**.
- **Check access rights** based on group memberships.
- **Troubleshoot permission issues** by confirming group assignments.

Syntax

```
groups
```

Syntax Explanation

- groups: Command to list all groups the current user belongs to.

Example

```
groups
```

Example Explanation

This command lists all groups the current user is a part of, such as pi, sudo, and others. Each group grants specific permissions based on system configuration.

Tip: To view another user's groups, use groups <username>.

Changing File Permissions

What is It?

The chmod command changes the access permissions of a file or directory. Permissions control who can read, write, or execute the file, allowing you to secure sensitive files.

Use

- **Control access to files** by specifying who can read, write, or execute them.
- **Set restrictive permissions** for sensitive files.
- **Manage shared files** by adjusting group and other user permissions.

Syntax

```
chmod <permissions> <file>
```

Syntax Explanation

- chmod: Changes file permissions.
- `<permissions>`: Specifies the permission levels (e.g., 755 or u+rwx).
- `<file>`: The file or directory to modify.

Example

```
chmod 755 myfile.txt
```

Example Explanation

This command sets `myfile.txt` to be readable and executable by everyone but only writable by the owner. 755 translates to `rwxr-xr-x`, meaning full access for the owner, and read and execute permissions for group and others.

Tip: Use `ls -l` to view current permissions on files.

Changing File Owner/Group

What is It?

The chown command changes the ownership of a file or directory. You can assign a new user or group to control access based on who owns the file.

Use

- **Transfer file ownership** to a specific user.
- **Assign group ownership** for shared access.
- **Control access** by setting appropriate ownership on sensitive files.

Syntax

```
chown <user>:<group> <file>
```

Syntax Explanation

- chown: Changes file owner and group.
- <user>: The new owner of the file.
- <group>: The new group for the file.
- <file>: The file or directory to modify.

Example

```
chown john:staff myfile.txt
```

Example Explanation

This command changes the owner of myfile.txt to john and the group to staff. Now, only john and members of the staff group have access based on the file's permissions.

Tip: Use ls -l to confirm ownership changes.

Configuring Privileges

What is It?

The sudo visudo command opens the sudoers file, which defines user permissions for executing commands with sudo. This file allows you to grant or restrict administrative privileges to specific users or groups.

Use

- **Grant administrative privileges** to users or groups.
- **Restrict sudo access** for security purposes.
- **Configure custom command access** for certain users.

Syntax

```
sudo visudo
```

Syntax Explanation

- sudo: Grants root privileges, required to edit the sudoers file.
- visudo: Opens the sudoers file in a safe editing mode to prevent syntax errors.

Example

```
sudo visudo
```

Example Explanation

Running sudo visudo opens the sudoers file in a text editor, allowing you to edit user privileges. You can add lines like john ALL=(ALL) NOPASSWD:ALL to grant john passwordless sudo access, or restrict sudo privileges as needed.

Tip: Avoid editing the sudoers file directly with other editors, as visudo includes syntax checking to prevent errors that could lock you out.

Chapter Conclusion

These user and permissions management commands provide essential tools for controlling access to your Raspberry Pi. By adding users, configuring group memberships, setting file permissions, and managing sudo privileges, you ensure a secure and organized system. Practice these commands to efficiently manage users, protect sensitive files, and control administrative access, creating a stable and secure environment for all users on your Raspberry Pi.

Chapter- 8 System Shutdown and Reboot

Chapter Overview

This chapter covers essential commands for shutting down and rebooting your Raspberry Pi safely. These commands allow you to restart, shut down, or halt the system, ensuring that your Raspberry Pi's processes are properly terminated to prevent data loss or corruption.

Chapter Purpose

- **Learn to safely shut down and reboot** the Raspberry Pi.
- **Understand when to use each command** for shutdown and reboot operations.
- **Manage system power** effectively to prevent data loss and ensure proper system maintenance.
- **Use commands with different options** for immediate or scheduled shutdowns.

Syntax Table

Topics	Syntax	Simple Example
Rebooting the System	sudo reboot	sudo reboot
Shutting Down Immediately	sudo shutdown now	sudo shutdown now
Halting the System	sudo shutdown -h now	sudo shutdown -h now
Restarting the System	sudo shutdown -r now	sudo shutdown -r now

Command Details

Rebooting the System

What is It?
The `sudo reboot` command restarts the Raspberry Pi, terminating all active processes and rebooting the system. This is useful if the system needs a fresh start, or if you've made configuration changes that require a reboot to take effect.

Use

- **Apply configuration changes** that require a reboot.
- **Restart the system** to resolve software or hardware issues.
- **Prepare the system** for consistent uptime after minor maintenance.

Syntax

```
sudo reboot
```

Syntax Explanation

- `sudo`: Grants root privileges, required for rebooting the system.
- `reboot`: Command to safely terminate active processes and restart the system.

Example

```
sudo reboot
```

Example Explanation
This command reboots the Raspberry Pi immediately. All running applications will be closed, and the system will restart, reloading the operating system and services.

Tip: Save any open files before running `sudo reboot` to avoid data loss.

Shutting Down Immediately

What is It?

The sudo shutdown now command shuts down the Raspberry Pi immediately, terminating all processes and powering down the system. This command is useful when you need to shut down quickly and safely.

Use

- **Power off the system** safely when it's no longer needed.
- **Shut down immediately** to perform maintenance or switch off the Pi.
- **Avoid data corruption** by properly shutting down instead of unplugging.

Syntax

```
sudo shutdown now
```

Syntax Explanation

- sudo: Executes the command with root privileges, necessary for system shutdown.
- shutdown: Command to power off the system.
- now: Shuts down the system immediately.

Example

```
sudo shutdown now
```

Example Explanation

This command shuts down the Raspberry Pi immediately. All processes are terminated, and the Pi powers off safely, preventing data corruption.

Tip: Wait for the green LED on your Pi to stop blinking before unplugging to ensure it's fully powered off.

Halting the System

What is It?

The sudo `shutdown -h` now command halts the Raspberry Pi, stopping all processes and powering down the system. Halting is similar to a shutdown but does not power off some systems. On the Raspberry Pi, it powers down fully.

Use

- **Stop all processes** without a reboot.
- **Prepare the Pi for safe power disconnection**.
- **Shutdown fully and securely** to avoid data corruption.

Syntax

```
sudo shutdown -h now
```

Syntax Explanation

- sudo: Executes the command with elevated privileges.
- shutdown: Initiates the process to stop all system operations.
- -h: Stands for "halt," indicating that the system should stop all processes.
- now: Executes the halt command immediately.

Example

```
sudo shutdown -h now
```

Example Explanation

This command halts the Raspberry Pi, stopping all processes and powering off the system. It's equivalent to a complete shutdown, ensuring all active processes are safely terminated.

Tip: Use shutdown -h <time> to schedule a halt at a specific time (e.g., shutdown -h 10:00 to halt at 10:00 AM).

Restarting the System

What is It?

The `sudo shutdown -r now` command immediately restarts the Raspberry Pi after terminating all processes, providing a safe way to restart without manually powering it down and back up.

Use

- **Reboot the system immediately** without needing to wait for scheduled reboots.
- **Apply updates or configurations** that require a restart.
- **Troubleshoot issues** by giving the system a fresh start.

Syntax

```
sudo shutdown -r now
```

Syntax Explanation

- sudo: Grants the necessary privileges for rebooting.
- shutdown: Command to safely terminate all processes.
- -r: Option to restart the system after shutdown.
- now: Executes the restart immediately.

Example

```
sudo shutdown -r now
```

Example Explanation

This command shuts down and immediately restarts the Raspberry Pi, safely closing all active applications and processes before rebooting.

Chapter Conclusion

These system shutdown and reboot commands are essential for managing your Raspberry Pi's power state safely. Using these commands ensures that all processes are terminated properly, reducing the risk of data corruption. Practice using these commands to shut down, halt, and reboot the system as needed, and remember to save your work before executing any shutdown or restart commands. These commands provide a safe and efficient way to manage your Raspberry Pi's power and maintenance requirements.

Chapter- 9 File Permissions and Security

Chapter Overview

This chapter focuses on commands for managing file permissions and securing your Raspberry Pi. These commands allow you to set permissions for files, enable the firewall, and check firewall status. Properly configuring file permissions and security settings is essential for protecting your data and ensuring that only authorized users have access.

Chapter Purpose

- **Learn to set and modify file permissions** for secure access control.
- **Enable and monitor firewall settings** to enhance network security.
- **Use permissions wisely** to control access levels for different users.
- **Protect your system** by understanding and applying best practices in permissions and security.

Syntax Table

Topics	Syntax	Simple Example
Making a Script Executable	chmod +x <script>	chmod +x myscript.sh
Enabling the Firewall	sudo ufw enable	sudo ufw enable
Checking Firewall Status	ufw status	ufw status
Setting Full Permissions	chmod 777 <file>	chmod 777 myfile.txt

Command Details

Making a Script Executable

What is It?
The chmod +x <script> command grants execute permissions to a specified script or file. This permission change allows the file to be run as a program or script directly from the command line.

Use

- **Enable scripts to be executable** directly from the command line.
- **Simplify script usage** by setting executable permissions.
- **Prepare files for running** without needing to specify an interpreter.

Syntax

```
chmod +x <script>
```

Syntax Explanation

- chmod: Changes the file permissions.
- +x: Grants execute permission to the file.
- <script>: The name of the script or file to make executable.

Example

```
chmod +x myscript.sh
```

Example Explanation
This command gives the myscript.sh file execute permissions, allowing it to be run directly with ./myscript.sh. Without +x, you would need to specify an interpreter (e.g., myscript.sh) to execute it.

Tip: Use `ls -l` to confirm the permission change, looking for x in the permissions column.

Enabling the Firewall

What is It?

The `sudo ufw enable` command enables the Uncomplicated Firewall (UFW) on your Raspberry Pi, providing an added layer of security by controlling incoming and outgoing network traffic.

Use

- **Activate firewall protection** to block unauthorized access.
- **Restrict network access** to specific ports or services.
- **Enhance security** by filtering traffic based on firewall rules.

Syntax

```
sudo ufw enable
```

Syntax Explanation

- sudo: Executes the command with root privileges, required for firewall configuration.
- ufw: Stands for Uncomplicated Firewall, a tool to manage iptables with simple commands.
- enable: Activates the firewall based on preconfigured rules.

Example

```
sudo ufw enable
```

Example Explanation

This command enables the firewall on your Raspberry Pi. Once activated, only permitted network connections are allowed. This is especially useful for securing the Pi in networked environments.

Tip: Use `sudo ufw allow <port>` to open specific ports (e.g., `sudo ufw allow 22` for SSH access).

Checking Firewall Status

What is It?
The `ufw status` command checks the current status of the firewall, showing whether it's enabled and listing any active rules.

Use

- **Verify firewall status** to ensure it's active.
- **Review active rules** to see which ports or services are allowed.
- **Monitor security settings** to confirm firewall protections are in place.

Syntax

```
ufw status
```

Syntax Explanation

- `ufw`: The Uncomplicated Firewall tool.
- `status`: Shows the firewall's current status and active rules.

Example

```
ufw status
```

Example Explanation
This command displays the status of the firewall (enabled or disabled) and any active rules that permit or deny network traffic. For instance, you might see entries like `22/tcp ALLOW` if SSH is allowed.

Setting Full Permissions
What is It?

The chmod 777 <file> command sets full permissions (read, write, and execute) for all users on a specified file. This permission level should be used sparingly and only for non-sensitive files, as it allows anyone with access to the file to read, modify, or execute it.

Use

- **Grant universal access** for public or shared files.
- **Enable full access** temporarily for troubleshooting.
- **Avoid restrictions** for files in shared or accessible directories.

Syntax

```
chmod 777 <file>
```

Syntax Explanation

- chmod: Command to change file permissions.
- 777: Grants full read, write, and execute permissions to all users (owner, group, and others).
- <file>: The file to apply full permissions to.

Example

```
chmod 777 myfile.txt
```

Example Explanation

This command gives all users full permissions on myfile.txt, allowing anyone to read, write, and execute it. This permission level is often used in public directories but should be avoided for sensitive files, as it poses a security risk.

Warning: Use chmod 777 carefully, as it can expose files to unauthorized modifications or misuse.

Chapter Conclusion

These file permissions and security commands are essential for protecting your Raspberry Pi's data and resources. By managing file permissions carefully, enabling and checking firewall settings, and using permissions wisely, you can enhance the security of your system. Practice these commands to control access to files, enable firewall protection, and understand when to use different permission levels to maintain a secure and organized environment on your Raspberry Pi.

Chapter- 10 Editing Files and Text

Chapter Overview

This chapter introduces fundamental commands for editing and manipulating text files on your Raspberry Pi. These commands allow you to create, edit, view, and search text within files, providing essential tools for managing configuration files, scripts, and other text-based documents.

Chapter Purpose

- **Learn to edit files** using text editors like Nano and Vim.
- **Display file contents** and search within files for specific text.
- **Modify file content** with text manipulation commands.
- **Master basic text processing** to efficiently manage files on the command line.

Syntax Table

Topics	Syntax	Simple Example
Editing with Nano	nano <filename>	nano myfile.txt
Editing with Vim	vim <filename>	vim myfile.txt
Writing Text to a File	echo "text" > <file>	echo "Hello, World!" > greeting.txt
Displaying File Content	cat <filename>	cat myfile.txt

Searching Within a File	grep "text" <file>	grep "error" logfile.txt
Replacing Text in a File	sed 's/old/new/g' <file>	sed 's/foo/bar/g' myfile.txt

Command Details

Editing with Nano

What is It?
The nano command opens a file in the Nano text editor, a beginner-friendly editor that operates directly in the terminal. It's ideal for quick edits and simple file management tasks.

Use

- **Edit configuration files** and scripts directly on the command line.
- **Add or modify text** without needing a graphical editor.
- **Save and exit easily** with on-screen keyboard shortcuts.

Syntax

```
nano <filename>
```

Syntax Explanation

- nano: Opens the Nano text editor.
- <filename>: The file to be edited; if it doesn't exist, a new file will be created.

Example

```
nano myfile.txt
```

Example Explanation

This command opens `myfile.txt` in Nano. You can type to add or change text, and use `Ctrl + X` to exit, Y to confirm changes, and `Enter` to save the file.

Tip: Basic shortcuts are displayed at the bottom of the Nano editor. For example, `Ctrl + O` saves the file, and `Ctrl + W` searches within the file.

Editing with Vim

What is It?

The `vim` command opens a file in Vim, a powerful text editor for advanced users. Vim has multiple modes (such as insert and command modes) and provides robust text manipulation tools.

Use

- **Edit and manipulate text** with advanced editing commands.
- **Script automation** and efficient text processing with complex commands.
- **Modify files extensively** once you're familiar with Vim's commands.

Syntax

```
vim <filename>
```

Syntax Explanation

- `vim`: Opens the Vim text editor.
- `<filename>`: The file to be edited; if it doesn't exist, a new file will be created.

Example

```
vim myfile.txt
```

Example Explanation

This command opens `myfile.txt` in Vim. Use `i` to enter insert mode and make changes, `Esc` to exit insert mode, and `:wq` to save and close the file.

Tip: Vim has a steep learning curve, but it's very efficient for users who become familiar with it. Beginners may prefer Nano.

Writing Text to a File

What is It?

The `echo "text" > <file>` command writes specified text to a file, replacing any existing content. This is a quick way to create files with a single line of text or overwrite file content.

Use

- **Create new files** with predefined content.
- **Overwrite existing files** with new text.
- **Log output** to a file when used in scripts.

Syntax

```
echo "text" > <file>
```

Syntax Explanation

- `echo`: Outputs the specified text.
- `"text"`: The text to be written to the file.
- `>`: Redirects the text output to the specified file, overwriting any existing content.
- `<file>`: The file to write the text to.

Example

```
echo "Hello, World!" > greeting.txt
```

Example Explanation

This command writes "Hello, World!" to greeting.txt, overwriting any existing content. If greeting.txt doesn't exist, it creates the file.

Tip: Use >> instead of > to append text to the file rather than overwriting it.

Displaying File Content

What is It?

The cat command displays the content of a file directly in the terminal. It's ideal for quickly viewing the contents of a small file without opening an editor.

Use

- **View file content** without editing.
- **Combine multiple files** by displaying them sequentially.
- **Verify changes** made to a file by viewing it immediately.

Syntax

```
cat <filename>
```

Syntax Explanation

- cat: Stands for "concatenate" but is commonly used to display file content.
- <filename>: The file to display.

Example

```
cat myfile.txt
```

Example Explanation

This command displays the entire content of `myfile.txt` in the terminal. It's especially useful for small files that fit within a single screen.

Tip: For large files, use `less` or `more` instead of `cat` to view content one screen at a time.

Searching Within a File

What is It?

The `grep` command searches for a specific text pattern within a file and displays matching lines. This is useful for locating specific information in log files or large text files.

Use

- **Search for keywords** or phrases in files.
- **Filter relevant information** from large files or logs.
- **Combine with other commands** for efficient text processing.

Syntax

```
grep "text" <file>
```

Syntax Explanation

- `grep`: Searches for text within files.
- `"text"`: The text or pattern to search for.
- `<file>`: The file to search within.

Example

```
grep "error" logfile.txt
```

Example Explanation

This command searches for the word "error" in logfile.txt and displays any lines containing that word, useful for identifying issues in log files.

Tip: Use grep -i "text" <file> to make the search case-insensitive.

Replacing Text in a File

What is It?

The sed 's/old/new/g' <file> command uses the sed (stream editor) tool to replace text within a file. This command replaces all instances of a specified word or phrase in the file, making it helpful for batch text replacements.

Use

- **Automate text replacements** in configuration or script files.
- **Edit multiple instances** of a word or phrase within a file.
- **Update file content quickly** without opening it in an editor.

Syntax

```
sed 's/old/new/g' <file>
```

Syntax Explanation

- sed: Command-line tool for stream editing.
- 's/old/new/g': Substitution pattern, where old is the text to replace, new is the replacement text, and g specifies global replacement (all instances).
- <file>: The file in which to replace text.

Example

```
sed 's/foo/bar/g' myfile.txt
```

Example Explanation
This command replaces every instance of "foo" with "bar" in
`myfile.txt`. It's a quick way to update multiple occurrences of a
word in a file.

Tip: To save changes directly to the file, use `sed -i`
`'s/old/new/g'` `<file>` (Linux-only, not supported by all
versions of sed).

Chapter Conclusion

These editing and text manipulation commands provide essential
tools for managing text files on your Raspberry Pi. By mastering
basic editors like Nano and Vim, learning to display and search file
content, and practicing text replacements with `sed`, you'll be able to
efficiently edit and process text files. Practice these commands
regularly to build confidence in file editing and text processing,
enabling you to handle a wide range of text-related tasks on the
command line.

Chapter- 11 Disk and Storage Management

Chapter Overview

This chapter introduces essential commands for managing disk space and storage devices on your Raspberry Pi. These commands allow you to view disk usage, check partition information, mount and unmount storage devices, and copy disk images. Understanding these tools is key to efficiently managing storage space and connected devices.

Chapter Purpose

- **Monitor available disk space** to prevent storage issues.
- **View directory sizes** to identify large files or folders.
- **Manage disk partitions** and understand device layout.
- **Mount and unmount devices** for external storage management.
- **Copy disk images** for backups and system cloning.

Syntax Table

Topics	Syntax	Simple Example
Checking Disk Space	df -h	df -h
Displaying Directory Size	du -sh <directory>	du -sh /home/pi/Documents
Listing Disk Partitions	fdisk -l	fdisk -l

Mounting a Device	`mount <device> <mount_point>`	`mount /dev/sda1 /mnt/usb`
Unmounting a Device	`umount <device>`	`umount /dev/sda1`
Copying Disk Images	`dd if=<source> of=<destination>`	`dd if=/dev/sda of=/path/image.img`

Command Details

Checking Disk Space
What is It?
The `df -h` command displays information about disk space usage on mounted filesystems, making it easy to check available storage and manage space effectively.
Use

- **Monitor available disk space** on each filesystem.
- **Identify disk usage trends** to prevent running out of space.
- **View human-readable sizes** (in GB, MB, etc.) for easier interpretation.

Syntax
```
df -h
```
Syntax Explanation
- `df`: Displays information about disk space usage.
- `-h`: Formats the output in human-readable sizes (e.g., GB, MB).

Example

```
df -h
```
Example Explanation
This command shows disk usage for each mounted filesystem, with columns for total size, used space, available space, and the percentage used. It's useful for quickly checking how much space is left on each drive.

Tip: Use df -hT to see the type of filesystem (e.g., ext4, vfat) alongside the disk usage.

Displaying Directory Size

What is It?
The du -sh <directory> command displays the size of a specified directory, allowing you to check which directories consume the most space.

Use

- **Check the size of folders** to manage storage effectively.
- **Identify large directories** for storage cleanup.
- **Monitor storage usage** in specific directories.

Syntax

```
du -sh <directory>
```

Syntax Explanation

- du: Displays disk usage.
- -s: Summarizes the total size of the directory.
- -h: Formats the output in human-readable units.
- <directory>: The directory to check.

Example
```
du -sh /home/pi/Documents
```
Example Explanation
This command shows the total size of the /home/pi/Documents directory. This information is helpful for identifying which folders use the most space on your system.

Tip: To list sizes for all subdirectories, use du -h /home/pi/Documents.

Listing Disk Partitions

What is It?

The `fdisk -l` command lists all disk partitions on your system, showing details like partition size, type, and device name. It's useful for identifying available storage devices and partition layouts.

Use

- **View partition details** for each disk.
- **Identify partition names** and sizes for mounting or troubleshooting.
- **Analyze storage layout** to understand available space and partitions.

Syntax

```
fdisk -l
```

Syntax Explanation

- `fdisk`: A command-line disk partitioning utility.
- `-l`: Lists all disk partitions on the system.

Example

```
fdisk -l
```

Example Explanation

This command displays a list of all partitions, including information such as device name (e.g., /dev/sda1), partition type (e.g., Linux, FAT32), and size. This information helps you identify partitions to mount, unmount, or modify.

Tip: Use `lsblk` as an alternative to `fdisk -l` for a tree view of disks and partitions.

Mounting a Device

What is It?

The `mount <device> <mount_point>` command attaches a storage device (e.g., USB drive) to a specific directory on your system, allowing access to the device's files.

Use

- **Access files on external devices** like USB drives or external hard drives.
- **Integrate external storage** into your filesystem.
- **Mount partitions** for system modifications or data access.

Syntax

```
mount <device> <mount_point>
```

Syntax Explanation

- `mount`: Attaches a storage device to a directory on the filesystem.
- `<device>`: The name of the device to mount (e.g., `/dev/sda1`).
- `<mount_point>`: The directory where the device will be accessible (e.g., `/mnt/usb`).

Example

```
mount /dev/sda1 /mnt/usb
```

Example Explanation

This command mounts the device `/dev/sda1` at the `/mnt/usb` directory, making the files on `/dev/sda1` accessible within `/mnt/usb`.

Tip: Use `sudo mkdir /mnt/usb` to create a mount point directory if it doesn't exist.

Unmounting a Device

What is It?

The umount <device> command detaches a mounted device from the filesystem. This is necessary before removing a device to avoid data corruption.

Use

- **Safely disconnect external storage** devices.
- **Prevent data loss** by unmounting devices properly before removal.
- **Free up the mount point** for other devices.

Syntax

```
umount <device>
```

Syntax Explanation

- umount: Detaches the specified device from the filesystem.
- <device>: The name of the device to unmount (e.g., /dev/sda1).

Example

```
umount /dev/sda1
```

Example Explanation

This command unmounts /dev/sda1, making it safe to physically disconnect the device. Proper unmounting helps prevent data corruption, especially for external USB drives.

Tip: If you receive a "device is busy" error, ensure no files are open from the device or try umount -l <device> for a lazy unmount.

Copying Disk Images

What is It?

The dd if=<source> of=<destination> command copies data from one location to another at the byte level. It's commonly used to create disk images or backup partitions.

Use

- **Create backups of entire disks or partitions**.
- **Clone disk images** for system replication or migration.
- **Restore disk images** from backups to a target drive.

Syntax

```
dd if=<source> of=<destination>
```

Syntax Explanation

- dd: A low-level copying command.
- if=<source>: The input file or source (e.g., /dev/sda).
- of=<destination>: The output file or destination (e.g., /path/to/backup.img).

Example

```
dd if=/dev/sda of=/path/image.img
```

Example Explanation

This command copies the entire /dev/sda device to image.img, creating a disk image of the source. This is useful for making full-disk backups or creating bootable images.

Warning: Be careful with dd, as it overwrites data without confirmation. Ensure that your input and output paths are correct.

Tip: Use dd if=/path/image.img of=/dev/sda to restore an image back to a device.

Chapter Conclusion

These disk and storage management commands provide essential tools for monitoring disk space, managing partitions, and handling external devices on your Raspberry Pi. By learning to check disk usage, mount and unmount devices, and use dd for disk imaging, you can effectively manage storage and backup data as needed. Practice these commands to build confidence in managing disk space and handling external storage, ensuring your Raspberry Pi remains organized and optimized.

Chapter- 12 GPIO and Hardware

Chapter Overview

This chapter introduces essential commands for managing GPIO (General Purpose Input/Output) pins and connected hardware on your Raspberry Pi. These commands allow you to read and set GPIO pin states, detect I2C devices, and manage hardware modules, providing the foundation for working with external components like sensors, LEDs, and motors.

Chapter Purpose

- **Learn to control GPIO pins** for interfacing with external hardware.
- **Set pins as inputs or outputs** to receive or send signals.
- **Scan for I2C devices** to connect sensors or modules.
- **Manage hardware modules** to ensure compatibility and functionality.

Syntax Table

Topics	Syntax	Simple Example
Viewing GPIO Pin Status	gpio readall	gpio readall
Setting Pin as Input/Output	gpio mode <pin> <in/out>	gpio mode 17 out
Setting Pin State	gpio write <pin> <1/0>	gpio write 17 1

Scanning for I2C Devices	i2cdetect -y 1	i2cdetect -y 1
Listing Loaded Modules	lsmod	lsmod

Command Details

Viewing GPIO Pin Status

What is It?
The gpio readall command displays a table with the current status of all GPIO pins on the Raspberry Pi. It shows each pin's mode, state, and available function, helping you understand the current GPIO configuration.

Use
- **Check the status of GPIO pins** before making changes.
- **Identify available pins** for connecting new devices.
- **Monitor pin states** to troubleshoot hardware connections.

Syntax
```
gpio readall
```

Syntax Explanation
- gpio: Command-line utility for controlling GPIO pins.
- readall: Option to display a complete overview of all GPIO pins.

Example
```
gpio readall
```

Example Explanation
This command outputs a table showing the status of each GPIO pin, including its mode (input or output) and current state (high or low). It helps you understand the current configuration of all pins at a glance.

Tip: Use gpio read <pin> to check the status of a specific pin if you only need information for one pin.

Setting Pin as Input/Output

What is It?

The `gpio mode <pin> <in/out>` command configures a specific GPIO pin as either an input or an output. Setting a pin as an input allows it to receive signals (e.g., from a sensor), while setting it as an output allows it to send signals (e.g., to an LED).

Use

- **Configure pins for input** to receive data from sensors or switches.
- **Set pins as output** to control components like LEDs, relays, or motors.
- **Prepare pins for specific tasks** in hardware projects.

Syntax

```
gpio mode <pin> <in/out>
```

Syntax Explanation

- `gpio`: Command-line tool for GPIO control.
- `mode`: Option to set the mode of a pin.
- `<pin>`: The pin number to configure.
- `<in/out>`: Specify in for input or out for output.

Example

```
gpio mode 17 out
```

Example Explanation

This command sets GPIO pin 17 as an output. You can now control pin 17's state (high or low) to operate an LED, motor, or another output device.

Tip: Use the Broadcom (BCM) pin numbering to ensure compatibility with `gpio` commands.

Setting Pin State

What is It?

The gpio write <pin> <1/0> command sets a GPIO pin's state to high (1) or low (0). A high state sends a 3.3V signal, while a low state sends 0V. This command is typically used for controlling LEDs, motors, and other hardware components.

Use

- **Turn components on or off** by setting pin states.
- **Control LED states** or trigger relays by sending high or low signals.
- **Send digital signals** to other components or devices.

Syntax

```
gpio write <pin> <1/0>
```

Syntax Explanation

- gpio: GPIO control command.
- write: Option to set a pin's output state.
- <pin>: The pin number to control.
- <1/0>: 1 sets the pin high, and 0 sets the pin low.

Example

```
gpio write 17 1
```

Example Explanation

This command sets GPIO pin 17 to high (3.3V), which can turn on an LED or trigger a relay connected to pin 17.

Tip: Always set a pin as output with gpio mode <pin> out before using gpio write to avoid errors.

Scanning for I2C Devices

What is It?

The `i2cdetect -y 1` command scans for connected I2C devices on the Raspberry Pi. I2C (Inter-Integrated Circuit) is a protocol used to communicate with external components like sensors and displays.

Use

- **Identify connected I2C devices** for setup and configuration.
- **Confirm device connections** before starting an I2C-based project.
- **Detect and troubleshoot** I2C connection issues.

Syntax

```
i2cdetect -y 1
```

Syntax Explanation

- `i2cdetect`: Utility for detecting I2C devices on the system.
- `-y`: Suppresses prompts for interactive confirmation.
- `1`: Specifies the I2C bus (usually 1 for Raspberry Pi).

Example

```
i2cdetect -y 1
```

Example Explanation

This command lists all I2C devices connected to bus 1 in a table format. Each device's address is shown in hexadecimal, helping you identify and configure devices like temperature sensors and OLED displays.

Tip: If the command returns an error, ensure that I2C is enabled in the Raspberry Pi Configuration tool.

Listing Loaded Modules
What is It?

The lsmod command lists all currently loaded kernel modules, providing information on active hardware drivers. It's useful for verifying that required modules for GPIO, I2C, SPI, or other hardware protocols are loaded.

Use

- **Check loaded modules** for GPIO, I2C, and other hardware support.
- **Verify active drivers** for connected hardware components.
- **Troubleshoot hardware issues** by confirming required modules.

Syntax

```
lsmod
```

Syntax Explanation

- lsmod: Lists all loaded kernel modules, displaying the module name, memory usage, and dependencies.

Example

```
lsmod
```

Example Explanation

This command outputs a list of all active kernel modules, showing which drivers are loaded to support hardware components. For example, i2c_bcm2835 and spi_bcm2835 indicate I2C and SPI support on Raspberry Pi hardware.

Tip: Use modprobe <module> to manually load a module if it's not already active (e.g., modprobe i2c_bcm2835).

Chapter Conclusion

These GPIO and hardware management commands are essential for interacting with physical components on your Raspberry Pi. By learning to set GPIO pin modes, control pin states, scan for I2C devices, and check loaded modules, you can confidently integrate external hardware like sensors, LEDs, and motors. Practice these commands to build hardware projects and expand your Raspberry Pi's capabilities, creating a solid foundation for interfacing with the physical world.

Chapter- 13 Remote Access

Chapter Overview

This chapter introduces essential commands for accessing and managing files on remote systems. By using SSH (Secure Shell) and related tools, you can securely connect to your Raspberry Pi from another device, transfer files, and synchronize directories. These commands are invaluable for managing your Raspberry Pi remotely.

Chapter Purpose

- **Learn to access your Raspberry Pi remotely** for easier management.
- **Transfer files over SSH** for secure file sharing and backups.
- **Synchronize directories** to keep files up to date across devices.
- **Use secure methods** for remote access and file management.

Syntax Table

Topics	Syntax	Simple Example
SSH Remote Connection	`ssh <username>@<host name or IP>`	`ssh pi@192.168.1.10`
Copying Files over SSH	`scp <source> <username>@<destination>`	`scp file.txt pi@192.168.1.10:/home/pi/`
Synchronizing Files	`rsync -av <source> <destination>`	`rsync -av /home/pi/Documents/ pi@192.168.1.10:/home/pi/backup/`

Command Details

SSH Remote Connection

What is It?
The ssh command allows you to securely connect to a remote system via SSH (Secure Shell). By using SSH, you can access your Raspberry Pi's command line from another device, making it easy to manage and control your Pi remotely.

Use

- **Access your Raspberry Pi remotely** from any compatible device.
- **Perform maintenance and updates** without needing physical access to the Pi.
- **Control your Pi** from anywhere on the network or, with proper configuration, over the internet.

Syntax

```
ssh <username>@<hostname or IP>
```

Syntax Explanation
- ssh: Command to establish a secure connection with the remote system.
- <username>: The username of the account on the remote device.
- <hostname or IP>: The hostname (e.g., raspberrypi.local) or IP address (e.g., 192.168.1.10) of the remote device.

Example
```
ssh pi@192.168.1.10
```

Example Explanation
This command connects you to the Raspberry Pi with IP address 192.168.1.10 as the user pi. After entering your password, you'll have full command-line access to the Raspberry Pi.

Tip: For added security, consider setting up SSH key-based authentication instead of using a password.

Copying Files over SSH

What is It?
The scp command copies files securely over SSH, allowing you to transfer files between your local system and a remote system. This command is useful for sharing documents, scripts, and configuration files with your Raspberry Pi.

Use

- **Transfer files to and from your Raspberry Pi** for backup or configuration.
- **Copy files over SSH** to ensure security during the transfer.
- **Manage files remotely** by copying them between systems.

Syntax
```
scp <source> <username>@<destination>
```
Syntax Explanation
- scp: Command for secure file copy over SSH.
- <source>: The file or directory to transfer.
- <username>: The username on the remote system.
- <destination>: The remote location where the file will be copied (e.g., 192.168.1.10:/path/to/destination).

Example
```
scp file.txt pi@192.168.1.10:/home/pi/
```
Example Explanation
This command copies file.txt from the local machine to the /home/pi/ directory on the Raspberry Pi with IP 192.168.1.10. You'll be prompted for the pi user's password on the remote device.

Tip: Use -r with scp to copy entire directories (e.g., scp -r folder pi@192.168.1.10:/home/pi/).

Synchronizing Files

What is It?

The `rsync` command synchronizes files between two directories, ensuring that the destination contains the same files as the source. With SSH, you can use `rsync` to keep files synchronized between your Raspberry Pi and another device, making it ideal for backups and file management.

Use

- **Backup important files** from your Raspberry Pi to another device.
- **Keep files synchronized** between systems with minimal bandwidth.
- **Transfer only changed files** to save time and network resources.

Syntax

```
rsync -av <source> <destination>
```

Syntax Explanation

- `rsync`: Command to synchronize files between directories.
- `-a`: Archive mode, which preserves permissions, timestamps, and other metadata.
- `-v`: Verbose mode, which displays progress during the synchronization.
- `<source>`: The directory to sync from.
- `<destination>`: The directory to sync to; this can be on a remote system.

Example

```
rsync -av /home/pi/Documents/
pi@192.168.1.10:/home/pi/backup/
```

Example Explanation

This command synchronizes the contents of
/home/pi/Documents/ from the local Raspberry Pi to the
/home/pi/backup/ directory on the remote Raspberry Pi at IP
192.168.1.10. Only new or changed files will be transferred,
making it efficient for regular backups.

Tip: Use --delete with rsync to remove files from the destination
that no longer exist in the source (e.g., rsync -av --delete
/home/pi/Documents/
pi@192.168.1.10:/home/pi/backup/).

Chapter Conclusion

These remote access commands provide essential tools for
managing your Raspberry Pi from a distance. By using SSH, SCP,
and rsync, you can access your Pi's command line, transfer files
securely, and synchronize directories, making it easy to maintain
and backup your Raspberry Pi. Practice these commands to build
confidence in managing your Pi remotely, ensuring you can control,
update, and protect your Raspberry Pi effectively from anywhere.

Chapter- 14 Advanced Networking

Chapter Overview

This chapter covers advanced networking commands for managing and troubleshooting network connections on your Raspberry Pi. These commands allow you to scan networks for open ports, view connected devices, trace network paths, and configure IP addresses, providing powerful tools for network diagnostics and security.

Chapter Purpose

- **Learn to scan networks** to identify connected devices and open ports.
- **Monitor open ports and active connections** for security and performance.
- **View and manage IP address configurations** to understand network settings.
- **Trace routes and view device addresses** for network troubleshooting and analysis.

Syntax Table

Topics	Syntax	Simple Example
Scanning for Open Ports	`nmap <IP or range>`	`nmap 192.168.1.1`
Showing Open Ports and Connections	`netstat -tuln`	`netstat -tuln`
Displaying IP Configuration	`ip addr`	`ip addr`
Tracing Route to Host	`traceroute <hostname>`	`traceroute google.com`
Viewing ARP Table	`arp -a`	`arp -a`

Command Details

Scanning for Open Ports

What is It?
The nmap command scans networks for open ports and connected devices, providing insight into which services are running on which ports. This command is useful for network security assessments and identifying active devices on a network.

Use

- **Identify devices and services** on a local network.
- **Check for open ports** on devices for security monitoring.
- **Assess network security** by scanning for unauthorized open ports.

Syntax

```
nmap <IP or range>
```

Syntax Explanation

- nmap: Network Mapper, a tool for scanning networks.
- <IP or range>: The IP address or range to scan (e.g., 192.168.1.1 or 192.168.1.0/24 for a subnet scan).

Example
```
nmap 192.168.1.1
```
Example Explanation
This command scans the device at 192.168.1.1 for open ports and active services. You can also scan an entire subnet, such as 192.168.1.0/24, to see all devices on the network.

Tip: Use nmap -sP <IP range> to perform a "ping scan" that lists active devices without scanning ports.

Showing Open Ports and Connections

What is It?
The `netstat -tuln` command shows open ports and active connections on the Raspberry Pi, providing insight into running services and their network usage. This command is valuable for monitoring network traffic and checking which applications are listening on specific ports.

Use

- **View all open ports** and their associated services.
- **Monitor active network connections** for performance and security.
- **Identify listening ports** to troubleshoot network-related issues.

Syntax

```
netstat -tuln
```

Syntax Explanation

- `netstat`: A network statistics command that shows open ports and connections.
- `-tuln`: Flags to display TCP and UDP connections in numeric format with listening ports.

Example

```
netstat -tuln
```
Example Explanation
This command lists all open ports and active connections on the Raspberry Pi, showing the protocol (TCP/UDP), local address, and port number. For example, `tcp 0 0 0.0.0.0:22` indicates that the SSH service is listening on port 22.

Tip: Use `ss -tuln` as an alternative to `netstat`, as `ss` provides similar information with a slightly different format.

Displaying IP Configuration

What is It?

The `ip addr` command displays detailed IP configuration information for each network interface on your Raspberry Pi. It shows the IP address, subnet mask, MAC address, and connection state of each interface.

Use

- **Check the IP address** assigned to each network interface.
- **Verify subnet and broadcast addresses** for network troubleshooting.
- **Monitor network interface states** to ensure proper connectivity.

Syntax

```
ip addr
```

Syntax Explanation

- `ip`: A command for IP configuration and network management.
- `addr`: Option to display IP address information for each interface.

Example

```
ip addr
```

Example Explanation

This command shows IP address details for all network interfaces, such as `eth0` (Ethernet) and `wlan0` (Wi-Fi). It includes information on the assigned IP address, MAC address, and interface state (e.g., UP or DOWN).

Tip: Use `ip -br addr` for a brief and easier-to-read format.

Tracing Route to Host

What is It?

The `traceroute` command traces the route that packets take to reach a specified host. This command shows each intermediate router or device along the path, helping to diagnose network delays and routing issues.

Use

- **Identify network bottlenecks** by viewing each hop to a destination.
- **Troubleshoot network delays** by analyzing response times at each hop.
- **Understand the route** traffic takes to reach a remote host.

Syntax

```
traceroute <hostname>
```

Syntax Explanation

- `traceroute`: Command to trace the network path to a specified host.
- `<hostname>`: The domain name or IP address of the destination.

Example

```
traceroute google.com
```

Example Explanation

This command traces the route from your Raspberry Pi to `google.com`, displaying each hop (intermediate device) along the way. Each line shows the IP address of the hop and the response time, which is useful for identifying slow or problematic network segments.

Tip: Use `traceroute -n <hostname>` to show only IP addresses (without resolving hostnames), which can speed up the output.

Viewing ARP Table
What is It?

The `arp -a` command displays the ARP (Address Resolution Protocol) table, which maps IP addresses to MAC addresses for devices on the local network. This table is helpful for identifying connected devices and their hardware (MAC) addresses.

Use

- **View IP and MAC addresses** of devices on your local network.
- **Identify connected devices** by IP or MAC address.
- **Troubleshoot local network issues** by confirming device connections.

Syntax

```
arp -a
```

Syntax Explanation

- `arp`: Command for viewing and managing the ARP table.
- `-a`: Lists all entries in the ARP table.

Example

```
arp -a
```

Example Explanation

This command lists the IP and MAC addresses of all devices recently interacted with on the local network, showing each device's IP address and its corresponding hardware address. This information is useful for identifying devices by MAC address or verifying connections on the network.

Tip: If a device does not appear in the ARP table, try pinging it first to update the ARP entries.

Chapter Conclusion

These advanced networking commands provide powerful tools for managing and troubleshooting network connections on your Raspberry Pi. By mastering nmap for port scanning, `netstat` for viewing connections, `ip addr` for IP configuration, `traceroute` for route tracking, and `arp` for mapping IPs to MACs, you can effectively diagnose and secure your network. Practice these commands to enhance your networking skills, gaining valuable insights into your Raspberry Pi's network interactions.

Chapter- 15 Log Management

Chapter Overview

This chapter introduces essential commands for viewing and monitoring system logs on your Raspberry Pi. These logs provide valuable information about system events, errors, hardware interactions, and user logins, making them crucial for troubleshooting and system management.

Chapter Purpose

- **Learn to monitor system logs in real-time** to detect issues as they occur.
- **Access detailed system logs** for deeper troubleshooting.
- **Review login history** to track user access and detect suspicious activity.
- **Examine hardware and kernel messages** for insights into hardware behavior.

Syntax Table

Topics	Syntax	Simple Example
Monitoring System Logs in Real-Time	`tail -f /var/log/syslog`	`tail -f /var/log/syslog`
Viewing Extended System Logs	`journalctl -xe`	`journalctl -xe`
Showing Last Logins	`last`	`last`
Displaying System Log	`cat /var/log/syslog`	`cat /var/log/syslog`

Viewing Kernel and Hardware Messages	dmesg	dmesg

Command Details

Monitoring System Logs in Real-Time

What is It?
The `tail -f /var/log/syslog` command displays the latest entries in the system log and updates in real-time as new entries are added. This command is useful for actively monitoring system activity and detecting issues as they happen.

Use

- **Monitor log entries in real-time** to catch errors or events as they occur.
- **Track system processes** during troubleshooting.
- **Observe logs for specific services** when starting or stopping them.

Syntax
```
tail -f /var/log/syslog
```
Syntax Explanation
- `tail`: Displays the last few lines of a file.
- `-f`: Follows the file in real-time, updating with new entries.
- `/var/log/syslog`: Path to the main system log file.

Example
```
tail -f /var/log/syslog
```
Example Explanation
This command shows the last few lines of the `syslog` file and continuously updates as new entries are added. It's helpful for monitoring events in real-time, such as service status changes or error messages.

Tip: Press `Ctrl + C` to stop monitoring.

Viewing Extended System Logs

What is It?

The `journalctl -xe` command displays extended system logs with detailed information about recent events, errors, and service status. It includes messages from the systemd journal, which is the central logging system for systemd-based Linux distributions.

Use

- **Review recent errors and warnings** in greater detail.
- **Troubleshoot service issues** with extended logs.
- **Analyze system events** with timestamps for better context.

Syntax

```
journalctl -xe
```

Syntax Explanation

- `journalctl`: Command for viewing systemd journal logs.
- `-x`: Provides additional explanations for log messages.
- `-e`: Shows the most recent entries.

Example

```
journalctl -xe
```

Example Explanation

This command displays recent system events with detailed log entries, including extra context for each event. It's especially helpful for troubleshooting issues related to systemd services.

Tip: Use `journalctl -b` to view logs from the current boot session, filtering out older entries.

Showing Last Logins

What is It?
The `last` command displays a list of the most recent logins on your Raspberry Pi, showing user names, login times, and IP addresses (if applicable). This command helps you track user access and identify any unusual login activity.

Use

- **Track user access** to the system.
- **Monitor login patterns** to detect unauthorized access.
- **Audit login history** for security and compliance.

Syntax

```
last
```

Syntax Explanation

- `last`: Command to list recent login sessions, including user name, IP address, and session duration.

Example

```
last
```

Example Explanation
This command displays a list of recent user logins, showing each session's start time, duration, and IP address if the login was remote. It helps you monitor who has accessed the system and when.

Tip: Use `last <username>` to view login history for a specific user.

Displaying System Log

What is It?

The cat /var/log/syslog command displays the content of the system log file. This file records general system activity, including messages from services and applications, making it useful for reviewing past events.

Use

- **Review recent system events** to diagnose issues.
- **Check messages from services and applications** for errors.
- **Analyze system behavior** over a longer period than real-time monitoring.

Syntax

```
cat /var/log/syslog
```

Syntax Explanation

- cat: Command to display the content of a file.
- /var/log/syslog: Path to the main system log file.

Example

```
cat /var/log/syslog
```

Example Explanation

This command displays the full content of the syslog file, showing system events, errors, and messages logged over time. This is helpful for reviewing system behavior or diagnosing issues after they occur.

Tip: Use grep with cat (e.g., cat /var/log/syslog | grep "error") to search for specific terms in the log.

Viewing Kernel and Hardware Messages
What is It?

The dmesg command displays messages generated by the Linux kernel, particularly those related to hardware devices and drivers. It's useful for diagnosing hardware issues and viewing events related to system startup.

Use

- **Check for hardware errors** or issues with connected devices.
- **View kernel messages** for insights into system behavior.
- **Troubleshoot startup issues** by reviewing boot messages.

Syntax

```
dmesg
```

Syntax Explanation

- dmesg: Command to display messages from the kernel ring buffer.

Example

```
dmesg
```

Example Explanation

This command displays a list of kernel messages, which includes information about hardware detection, drivers, and kernel events. It's useful for identifying issues with USB devices, network adapters, and other hardware components.

Tip: Use dmesg | tail to view only the most recent kernel messages.

Chapter Conclusion

These log management commands provide essential tools for monitoring and troubleshooting system events on your Raspberry Pi. By learning to monitor logs in real-time, review extended logs, track login history, and examine kernel messages, you can effectively maintain your system and identify potential issues early. Practice these commands to develop confidence in log management and system diagnostics, ensuring a stable and well-maintained Raspberry Pi.

Chapter- 16 Development Tools

Chapter Overview

This chapter introduces essential development tools and commands for programming and software development on your Raspberry Pi. These commands allow you to compile C code, run Python scripts, build software, manage code with Git, and install Python packages, making your Raspberry Pi a powerful environment for development projects.

Chapter Purpose

- **Compile and run code** on your Raspberry Pi.
- **Use Makefiles to manage builds** for complex software projects.
- **Clone repositories** from GitHub or other sources for collaborative development.
- **Install Python packages** to expand the functionality of your Python projects.

Syntax Table

Topics	Syntax	Simple Example
Compiling C Code	`gcc <file>.c -o <output>`	`gcc hello.c -o hello`
Running a Python Script	`python3 <file>.py`	`python3 script.py`

Building with Makefile	`make`	`make`
Cloning a Git Repository	`git clone <repository_url>`	`git clone https://github.com/user/repo.git`
Installing Python Packages	`pip install <package>`	`pip install requests`

Command Details

Compiling C Code
What is It?

The gcc command is used to compile C programs. You can specify the input C file and output executable file name, allowing you to turn source code into a runnable application on your Raspberry Pi.

Use

- **Compile C programs** for development projects.
- **Create executable files** from source code.
- **Develop applications** and scripts that run directly on your Pi.

Syntax

```
gcc <file>.c -o <output>
```

Syntax Explanation

- gcc: GNU Compiler Collection, used for compiling C code.
- <file>.c: The C source file to compile.
- -o <output>: Specifies the name of the output executable file.

Example

```
gcc hello.c -o hello
```

Example Explanation

This command compiles hello.c and creates an executable file named `hello`. You can then run the compiled program with `./hello`.

Tip: For more complex programs with multiple files, use gcc with all file names (e.g., `gcc file1.c file2.c -o program`).

Running a Python Script

What is It?

The `python3` command runs Python scripts written in Python 3, allowing you to execute Python code directly from the command line. This command is essential for developing and testing Python programs.

Use

- **Run Python scripts** for development and testing.
- **Execute programs** created with Python.
- **Develop and test code interactively** in the command line environment.

Syntax

```
python3 <file>.py
```

Syntax Explanation

- `python3`: The Python 3 interpreter, which executes Python code.
- `<file>.py`: The Python file to run.

Example

```
python3 script.py
```

Example Explanation

This command runs `script.py` using Python 3, executing any code within the file. It's useful for testing and running Python applications on your Raspberry Pi.

Tip: Use `python3 -i <file>.py` to enter interactive mode after the script finishes running.

Building with Makefile

What is It?
The `make` command builds software projects based on instructions in a Makefile, a file that specifies how the project should be compiled and linked. Makefiles simplify the build process, especially for larger projects with multiple source files.

Use

- **Automate the build process** for software projects.
- **Compile multi-file projects** with a single command.
- **Manage dependencies** for complex applications.

Syntax

```
make
```

Syntax Explanation

- `make`: Reads the Makefile in the current directory and builds the project as specified.

Example

```
make
```

Example Explanation
If there's a Makefile in the current directory, this command compiles the project according to the rules defined in the Makefile, making it easy to build large applications.

Tip: Use `make clean` if defined in the Makefile, to remove build files and start fresh.

Cloning a Git Repository

What is It?

The `git clone` command copies a repository from a remote source (e.g., GitHub) to your local machine, allowing you to download and work with projects stored in Git repositories. This command is essential for collaborative development and accessing code from other developers.

Use

- **Download source code** from remote repositories.
- **Collaborate on projects** by cloning shared repositories.
- **Access open-source projects** hosted on platforms like GitHub.

Syntax

```
git clone <repository_url>
```

Syntax Explanation

- `git`: Command-line tool for interacting with Git repositories.
- `clone`: Clones (downloads) a repository from a remote URL.
- `<repository_url>`: The URL of the repository to clone.

Example

```
git clone https://github.com/user/repo.git
```

Example Explanation

This command clones the repository at

`https://github.com/user/repo.git` to your local machine, creating a directory named `repo` containing the project files.

Tip: Use `git pull` within a cloned repository to fetch the latest updates from the remote source.

Installing Python Packages
What is It?
The `pip install <package>` command installs Python packages from the Python Package Index (PyPI), enabling you to add libraries and modules to your Python environment. This is essential for using third-party libraries in Python projects.
Use
- **Install packages and libraries** for Python development.
- **Expand Python functionality** with pre-built modules.
- **Set up dependencies** required by specific Python applications.

Syntax
```
pip install <package>
```
Syntax Explanation
- `pip`: Python's package installer for downloading and managing libraries.
- `install`: Option to install the specified package.
- `<package>`: The name of the package to install.

Example
```
pip install requests
```
Example Explanation
This command installs the `requests` library, a popular package for handling HTTP requests in Python, making it available for use in Python scripts.

Chapter Conclusion

These development tools provide essential functionality for programming on your Raspberry Pi. By mastering `gcc` for compiling, `python3` for running Python scripts, `make` for building projects, `git clone` for managing repositories, and `pip` for installing packages, you can efficiently develop, test, and manage software projects. Practice these commands to create a versatile development environment on your Ras

Chapter- 17 Time and Localization

Chapter Overview

This chapter introduces essential commands for viewing and managing time, date, and localization settings on your Raspberry Pi. These commands allow you to display the current time, set the correct time zone, and configure language and regional settings, ensuring that your Raspberry Pi reflects accurate time and localization information.

Chapter Purpose

- **View the current date and time** to check system time.
- **Manage time zone and synchronization** to ensure accurate time.
- **Configure localization settings** for language, currency, and regional preferences.

Syntax Table

Topics	Syntax	Simple Example
Displaying Date and Time	date	date

Managing Date, Time, and Time Zone	timedate ctl	timedatectl
Displaying Localization Settings	locale	locale

Command Details

Displaying Date and Time

What is It?

The date command displays the current date and time according to your Raspberry Pi's system clock. This command is useful for quickly checking the current time and ensuring it matches the actual time.

Use

- **View the current date and time** on your Raspberry Pi.
- **Check if the system time is accurate**.
- **Verify time after changes** to system or time zone settings.

Syntax

```
date
```

Syntax Explanation

- date: A command to display the current date and time in a readable format.

Example

```
date
```

Example Explanation

This command outputs the current date and time, including day, month, year, and time in hours, minutes, and seconds. For example, you might see something like Wed Nov 10 12:34:56 UTC 2024.

Tip: Use date "+%Y-%m-%d %H:%M:%S" to customize the output format.

Managing Date, Time, and Time Zone

What is It?
The timedatectl command is a powerful tool for managing time, date, and time zone settings. It allows you to view the current configuration, change the time zone, and enable or disable network time synchronization.

Use

- **View current time, date, and time zone** settings.
- **Set the correct time zone** based on your location.
- **Enable automatic time synchronization** for accurate timekeeping.

Syntax

```
timedatectl
```

Syntax Explanation

- timedatectl: A command to manage system time and date settings, including time zone and synchronization.

Example

```
timedatectl
```

Example Explanation
This command displays the current time and date configuration,

including time zone and whether network time synchronization is active. You'll see entries for `Local time`, `Universal time` (UTC), `RTC time`, and `Time zone`.

Setting a Time Zone
To change the time zone, use:

```
sudo timedatectl set-timezone <Region/City>
```

For example:

```
sudo timedatectl set-timezone America/New_York
```

Enabling Network Time Synchronization
To enable automatic synchronization, use:

```
sudo timedatectl set-ntp true
```

Tip: Use `timedatectl list-timezones` to see a list of available time zones.

Displaying Localization Settings

What is It?
The `locale` command displays the current localization settings, including language, country, and regional preferences. Localization settings control formats for dates, numbers, currency, and more, ensuring that your system displays information according to regional conventions.

Use

- **View current language and regional settings** for your Raspberry Pi.
- **Confirm localization configuration** for language, currency, and measurement units.
- **Troubleshoot localization issues** by verifying the current settings.

Syntax

```
locale
```

Syntax Explanation

- `locale`: A command to display localization (locale) settings for language and regional formats.

Example

```
locale
```

Example Explanation
This command displays the current localization settings, including LANG (language), LC_TIME (date and time format), LC_MONETARY (currency format), and others. Each variable shows the configured language and region, such as en_US.UTF-8 for US English.

Tip: To change the locale settings, use sudo raspi-config and navigate to "Localisation Options" for a user-friendly configuration interface.

Chapter Conclusion

These time and localization commands are essential for managing date, time, and regional settings on your Raspberry Pi. By mastering date for displaying time, timedatectl for managing time zone and synchronization, and locale for viewing regional settings, you can ensure that your Raspberry Pi's time and format settings are accurate and match your preferences. Practice these commands to maintain correct and consistent time and localization settings on your device.

Chapter- 18 Audio and Bluetooth

Chapter Overview

This chapter introduces essential commands for managing audio and Bluetooth settings on your Raspberry Pi. These commands allow you to adjust audio volume, play audio files, control Bluetooth connections, and use a mixer interface for advanced audio settings, making it easy to configure and use audio and Bluetooth devices.

Chapter Purpose

- **Adjust audio settings** to control playback and volume.
- **Play audio files** directly from the command line.
- **Manage Bluetooth connections** for pairing and device control.
- **Use an audio mixer interface** for advanced audio adjustments.

Syntax Table

Topics	Syntax	Simple Example
Adjusting Audio Settings	`amixer`	`amixer set Master 50%`
Playing an Audio File	`aplay <file>.wav`	`aplay sound.wav`
Managing Bluetooth Connections	`bluetoothctl`	`bluetoothctl`

Opening Audio Mixer Interface	`alsamixer`	`alsamixer`

Command Details

Adjusting Audio Settings

What is It?

The `amixer` command adjusts audio settings on your Raspberry Pi, such as volume level and audio output device. This command is useful for controlling audio playback and managing volume from the command line.

Use

- **Increase or decrease volume** for audio playback.
- **Mute or unmute audio** as needed.
- **Select audio output device** (e.g., headphones, HDMI, or Bluetooth).

Syntax

```
amixer set <control> <value>
```

Syntax Explanation

- `amixer`: ALSA (Advanced Linux Sound Architecture) mixer control command.
- `set <control>`: Specifies the control to adjust (e.g., `Master` for master volume).
- `<value>`: The value to set, such as a percentage (e.g., 50%).

Example

```
amixer set Master 50%
```

Example Explanation

This command sets the master volume to 50% on your Raspberry

Pi. You can also use amixer set Master mute or amixer set Master unmute to mute or unmute the audio.

Playing an Audio File

What is It?
The aplay command plays WAV audio files directly from the command line. It's a simple and quick way to test audio playback without needing a full audio player application.

Use

- **Play WAV audio files** for quick testing.
- **Verify audio output** by playing a test sound.
- **Check connected audio devices** to ensure they are working.

Syntax

```
aplay <file>.wav
```

Syntax Explanation

- aplay: ALSA sound player for playing WAV files.
- <file>.wav: The path to the WAV file you want to play.

Example

```
aplay sound.wav
```

Example Explanation
This command plays the sound.wav file through the Raspberry Pi's audio output. It's useful for verifying that the audio output is working as expected.

Tip: Ensure the audio file is in WAV format, as aplay does not support other formats.

Managing Bluetooth Connections

What is It?
The `bluetoothctl` command provides an interactive command-line interface for managing Bluetooth devices. It allows you to scan, pair, connect, and disconnect Bluetooth devices from the Raspberry Pi.

Use

- **Pair and connect Bluetooth devices** like speakers, keyboards, or phones.
- **Scan for nearby Bluetooth devices** to connect to new devices.
- **Remove paired devices** when they are no longer needed.

Syntax

```
bluetoothctl
```

Syntax Explanation

- `bluetoothctl`: Opens the Bluetooth control interface.

Example

```
bluetoothctl
```

Example Explanation
This command opens the interactive `bluetoothctl` interface, where you can enter additional commands to manage Bluetooth devices, such as `scan` on to find nearby devices, `pair <device address>` to pair with a device, and `connect <device address>` to connect.

Basic Bluetooth Commands in bluetoothctl

- `scan on` – Starts scanning for available Bluetooth devices.
- `pair <device address>` – Pairs with a device using its address.
- `connect <device address>` – Connects to a paired device.
- `disconnect <device address>` – Disconnects a device.
- `remove <device address>` – Removes a paired device.

Tip: Use `bluetoothctl -- help` within the interface to see a list of available commands.

Opening Audio Mixer Interface

What is It?
The `alsamixer` command opens an interactive audio mixer interface, providing a graphical view in the terminal to control volume and other audio settings for various devices.

Use

- **Adjust individual audio settings** for different audio channels.
- **Control volume levels** with a graphical interface in the terminal.
- **Configure input and output devices** for advanced audio management.

Syntax

```
alsamixer
```

Syntax Explanation

- `alsamixer`: Opens the ALSA audio mixer interface, allowing you to adjust settings interactively.

Example

```
alsamixer
```

Example Explanation

This command opens the `alsamixer` interface, where you can adjust the volume, balance, and other audio settings. You can navigate the interface using arrow keys and press Esc to exit.

Tip: Use F6 within `alsamixer` to switch between audio devices.

Chapter Conclusion

These audio and Bluetooth commands provide essential tools for managing sound and Bluetooth connections on your Raspberry Pi. By mastering `amixer` for adjusting audio, `aplay` for playing audio files, `bluetoothctl` for managing Bluetooth devices, and `alsamixer` for advanced audio control, you can customize and optimize audio and Bluetooth functionality. Practice these commands to build confidence in managing audio playback and Bluetooth connections on your Raspberry Pi, ensuring a smooth experience with connected devices and sound output.

Chapter- 19 Additional Tools and Commands

Chapter Overview

This chapter covers essential additional commands that improve your command-line experience on the Raspberry Pi. These commands are helpful for managing your terminal environment, accessing past commands, and configuring basic settings through the Raspberry Pi configuration tool.

Chapter Purpose

- Clear the terminal screen for a tidy workspace.
- Access a list of previously used commands for easy reference.
- Open the Raspberry Pi configuration tool for adjusting basic settings.

Syntax Table

Topics	Syntax	Simple Example
Clearing the Terminal Screen	`clear`	`clear`
Listing Command History	`history`	`history`
Opening Configuration Tool	`raspi-config`	`raspi-config`

Command Details

Clearing the Terminal Screen

What is It?

The clear command is a simple command that clears the terminal screen, removing all previous output. This is useful for keeping your workspace organized, especially when working with multiple commands and outputs.

Use

- Clear the screen to create a clean workspace.
- Remove cluttered outputs, allowing focus on new commands.

Syntax

```
clear
```

Syntax Explanation

- **clear**: The command itself with no additional options, simply executed to wipe the terminal view.

Example

```
clear
```

Example Explanation

This command clears all text and previous output from the terminal screen, providing a blank space for continued work.

Listing Command History

What is It?

The `history` command displays a list of previously executed commands in the current terminal session. This is helpful for referencing past commands, reusing them, or identifying errors.

Use

- Access and review recently used commands.
- Re-run specific commands without retyping.
- Identify frequently used commands to streamline tasks.

Syntax

```
history
```

Syntax Explanation

- **`history`**: The command itself, which outputs a numbered list of commands used in the session.

Example

```
history
```

Example Explanation

This command displays a list of past commands in the current terminal session. You can also re-run any previous command by typing ! <number>, where <number> corresponds to the command number shown in the list.

Opening Configuration Tool

What is It?

The `raspi-config` command opens the Raspberry Pi configuration tool, which provides a menu-based interface to set up your Raspberry Pi's essential settings. It is especially useful for beginners to configure options without needing extensive command-line knowledge.

Use

- Adjust settings like localization, Wi-Fi, and password.
- Enable or disable hardware interfaces (e.g., GPIO, I2C, SPI).
- Set up networking, expand file system, and configure boot options.

Syntax

```
raspi-config
```

Syntax Explanation

- `raspi-config`: Launches the configuration tool with an easy-to-navigate menu interface.

Example

```
raspi-config
```

Example Explanation

This command opens the Raspberry Pi configuration tool, displaying a menu with various setup options. Use arrow keys to navigate the menu and Enter to select options. This tool is ideal for quickly configuring system settings without needing specific commands for each setting.

Chapter Conclusion

These additional tools and commands simplify everyday tasks on the Raspberry Pi by providing convenient ways to manage the terminal environment, access command history, and configure the system settings. By using `clear` to manage your terminal view, `history` to track your command usage, and `raspi-config` to handle basic configurations, you'll find it easier to maintain an organized and efficient workflow on your Raspberry Pi. Practice these commands to get comfortable with managing your workspace and system settings as you continue to work with your device.

www.ingramcontent.com/pod-product-compliance
Lightning Source LLC
LaVergne TN
LVHW051653050326
832903LV00032B/3784

* 9 7 9 8 3 4 6 1 9 5 0 5 4 *